THE **shaker** GARDEN

THE shaker GARDEN

beauty through utility

stephanie donaldson

David & Charles

A DAVID & CHARLES BOOK

First published in the UK in 2000
First published in paperback 2003
Copyright text © Stephanie Donaldson 2000, 2003
Copyright photographs © Michelle Garrett 2000
except page 63 © B & B Photographs/
Stefan Buczacki

Distributed in North America
by F&W Publications, Inc.
4700 East Galbraith Road
Cincinnati, OH 45236
1-800-289-0963

Stephanie Donaldson has asserted her right to be
identified as author of this work in accordance
with the Copyright, Designs and Patents Act, 1988.

A catalogue record for this book is available from
the British Library.

ISBN 0 7153 1610 9 paperback

BOOK DESIGN: Debbie Mole
PHOTOGRAPHY: Michelle Garrett
ILLUSTRATION: Gabrielle Izen
COMMISSIONING EDITOR: Anna Mumford
PROJECT EDITOR: Jane Trollope
EDITOR: Judith Walker Hodge

Printed in Singapore by KHL Printing Co Pte Ltd
for David & Charles
Brunel House, Newton Abbot, Devon

Visit our website at www.davidandcharles.co.uk

David & Charles books are available from all
good bookshops; alternatively you can contact
our Orderline on (0)1626 334555 or write to
us at FREEPOST EX2 110, David & Charles
Direct, Newton Abbot, TQ12 4ZZ (no stamp
required UK mainland).

Contents

Introduction

IF YOU LOVE THE PLANT and take heed of what it likes,

you will be well repaid by it.

ELDER FREDERICK EVANS

I HAVE LONG ADMIRED the pared down simplicity of Shaker architecture and design. Over the years as I have learnt more about the Shakers, I have found myself increasingly admiring of their approach to gardening, with its simple symmetry, use of natural materials and emphasis on useful beauty. While most of you will probably have felt their influence in your homes, you may not be aware of just how influential the Shakers have been in horticulture and agriculture.

Unlike the Amish they have never shunned innovation, and they readily adopted, and even invented, many labour-saving devices. This book is an interpretation of the Shaker principles of gardening rather than an exercise in historical accuracy. There are former Shaker settlements, now

left

New Shaker garden

The Shaker garden which was planted for this book was laid out according to Shaker principles.

centre

Plant supports

Pea sticks stand propped against the fence ready to be used.

right

Planting out

Seed potatoes and young runner bean plants are ready to be planted out.

run as museums in a number of locations in New England, Kentucky and Ohio where you can see modern versions of Shaker gardens in their original landscapes and I would not presume to attempt an imitation of them.

Instead I have laid out, cultivated and planted my own 'Shaker' garden using *The Gardener's Manual*, published in 1843, as my guide. I wanted to see how relevant their gardening techniques were to today's gardeners. In the process of doing this I realised that, in our modern world, where 'instant' is desirable and patience is forgotten, the Shakers have much to teach us about experiencing the processes of gardening and not just the results. They believed that every task undertaken should be done to the very best of their

abilities, and while their motivation was religious, one does not need a religious faith to adapt this practice to one's own garden. To plan carefully, dig thoroughly, plant with care and tend the plants regularly is the essence of good gardening.

There is an emphasis on growing productive plants, but by choosing the most decorative varieties, and combining flowers, fruit and vegetables, the garden is good to look at as well as a plentiful source of food. The use of efficient, well-made tools is common sense. Now that the love affair with indestructible plastic is receding, we have begun once more to appreciate the appearance of natural materials such as wood, stone and terracotta for pathways, fences, edgings, plant supports and containers.

left

Summer abundance

By mid-summer the structure of the garden was completely hidden by the rapidly growing fruit and vegetables.

right

On a smaller scale

In the miniature Shaker garden dwarf sunflowers grew amongst vegetables – once they had finished flowering their seed heads were dried for the birds.

In writing this book, it is not my intention that gardens should be remade in the Shaker image. It is rather that the principles of good organic gardening as practised by the Shakers should inspire readers to create simple, sustainable beauty wherever they garden and however large or small their gardens may be. Over the years I have come to understand that there are always two strands to gardening – good husbandry and fashion. Good husbandry is based on knowledge, experience and the passing of time, while fashion is far more fleeting. To the best of my ability *The Shaker Garden* is a book about good husbandry, inspired and informed by the Shaker Brothers and Sisters who gardened with no thought to fashion but with a deep understanding and love of plants.

STEPHANIE DONALDSON

above

Miniature garden

*Not everyone has the
space or the time to lay
out a proper vegetable
garden, but room could
easily be found for this
tiny garden which has
pot-grown plants arranged
within its boundaries and
then mulched with
composted bark.*

left

Shaker garden

*In its first year the Shaker
garden was wonderfully
productive, supplying some
fresh vegetables every day
from the time when it
started cropping. At times
there was more than
enough for the family, and
friends were delighted to
receive baskets of produce.*

History

Do all your work as though you had a thousand years to live, and as you would if you knew you must die tomorrow.

Mother Ann Lee

MOTHER ANN'S VISIONS

The Shaker movement began in Manchester, England. Believed to originate in a group of French prophets known as Camisards who fled to England to escape persecution, they became known as the 'Shaking Quakers' because of the ecstatic trembling that formed part of their worship. In 1758 an illiterate 22 year-old factory worker called Ann Lee joined the sect with James and Jane Wardley. Despite her lack of education, her strong religious beliefs and charismatic personality soon brought her to prominence.

left

Shaker women

Right from the beginning of the movement which was founded by Ann Lee, women were equals in the Shaker movement – although most of the time men and women lived and worked separately.

In 1770 when she was 34, she was imprisoned for her beliefs and experienced a vision that revealed to her that carnality was the cause of most of the world's problems. This vision was in all likelihood fuelled by the deaths of all four of her children by the time she was 30 years old. On the basis of this revelation she set out to preach a new way of life where men and women would live (preferably celibate) equal lives alongside one another. Other members of the sect followed her teaching and in time she became their leader. Her husband was far from happy with their new relationship, but he did accompany her, with seven other followers, when a further

revelation told her to sail for America in 1774. They experienced many hardships in the early years, living in great poverty and before long Ann Lee's husband left her, unable to share her commitment to celibacy or her belief in their future.

THE FIRST COMMUNITIES

In 1776 the Shakers, by then also known as the United Society of Believers in the First and Second Appearance of Christ, bought their first piece of land at Watervliet near Albany, New York, but even here things did not go well. Their first communal home built three years later, burnt down, and after five years they had only a handful of converts. However, in the spring of 1780 a religious revival resulted in many conversions and although 'Mother' Ann died in 1784, the surviving Shakers determined to continue her teachings. At the time of her death they still lived in 'the World', as they called society in general, but her appointed successors set about creating communal settlements where everything was jointly owned by the members. They

top left

Dwelling house

Within each settlement there were a number of dwelling houses which housed the Brothers and Sisters – sometimes under the same roof, but with separate entrances and staircases.

top right

Shaker elements

Attention to detail was central to the Shaker philosophy – no thing was too small for its detail to matter.

further developed the characteristics we now attribute to Shakerism, including obligatory celibacy.

BECOMING A SHAKER

The Shakers were not interested in hasty conversions, so commitment was planned as a gradual rather than an immediate process. To become a Shaker, individuals had to be at least 21 years old, have the permission of a spouse and be free of debt or obligations. They signed a covenant donating their personal property and agreeing to the rules, which included working for the mutual good and accepting the authority of the Society.

Within each community there would also be those considering membership and some who did not intend joining but were in need of a place to stay. They would contribute by bringing useful skills and knowledge to the community and earn their keep. Children were an important part of each 'Family' – children of members born prior to their parents becoming Shakers, those indentured by parents unable to care for them and orphans. The children went to school for four months

each year, girls in the summer and boys in the winter.

For women the Shaker way of life must have been particularly attractive. It freed them from the endless round of child-bearing and gave them an equal role in community life, as well as a comfortable home, security and good food. Although equal, men and women lived mainly separate lives. 'Family' members of both sexes often lived under the same roof, but entered through separate entrances, used different staircases and lived much of their life apart from one another except at mealtimes, worship or supervised meetings.

A TIME OF PROSPERITY

New Lebanon was the first of the utopian settlements established by the Shakers and was the model for the others that followed on. At their peak, the Shakers were the largest and most successful of all the communistic societies in America. Between 1787 and 1836, 22 Shaker communities were established in New England, Ohio, Kentucky and Indiana, each owning several thousand acres

above left

Meeting House

The Meeting House was the pivotal building where worship and meetings took place. It was the heart of the community.

above

Shaker details

Every building within the Shaker village had a designated use, reflecting the orderliness which existed at all levels within each community.

of land. Each community consisted of a number of 'Families' who built their own Meeting Houses, dwelling houses and ancillary buildings and lived independent, self-sufficient lives.

After the early, difficult years, this was a period of great prosperity for the Shakers. They lived simply but well, and as word spread in 'the World' of the quality of their workmanship and produce, they were able to establish very successful businesses, including the gathering and processing of medicinal herbs and seed growing. At its peak the seed business generated an enormous amount of money for the various communities – New Lebanon earned $10,000 in seed sales in 1853. *The Gardener's Manual,* first published in 1836, was an off-shoot of the seed business, intended to promote the sale of Shaker seeds and encourage good husbandry among the gardeners of 'the World', who until that time had received very little guidance on how to cultivate their gardens. The Shakers' advertising and marketing of their produce was always skillfully done.

Shaker gardens

THEY HAVE AN EXTENSIVE orchard, containing a great variety of excellent fruit, large medical and seed gardens, which are in fine order. These gardens are very profitable, as their herbs and seeds are everywhere sought after and purchased, being always esteemed better than any other which can be procured. They take great pains in drying and packing their medical herbs, and so highly are they valued that they have frequent orders for them from Europe to a very large amount.

PECULIARITIES OF THE SHAKERS 1832

EVERYONE WORKED according to his or her ability. Sisters ran the domestic side of things, milked the cows, preserved fruit and vegetables, gathered herbs and seeds and processed them. Brothers tended the crops and gardens. 'Aged Brethren' and those suffering from physical or mental infirmities, and boys too young for other work were sent to help in the garden. As their work needed constant supervision this was not always a popular arrangement among the head gardeners.

The Shakers were meticulous at recording everything about their gardens. Their almanacs recorded both their spiritual and working lives and frequently drew comparisons between the state of their souls and the state of their gardens.

By recording annual occurrences (phenology), they were able to judge the

right

The orderly garden

The gardens were essential food factories for the Shakers and were laid out for maximum productivity and efficiency to ensure that everyone would be well fed.

best time to carry out each task. For example, it was recommended that corn be planted when an oak leaf was the size of a squirrel's ear. Their success as gardeners was due to an equal measure of good practice and their spiritual goal of perfection. They did not strive for perfection for aesthetic reasons, although they had clear ideas on how things should look. Attention to detail was central – *'No one should carelessly pass over small things, as a pin, a kernel of grain, etc., thinking it too small to pick up, for if we do, our Heavenly Father will consider us too small for him to bestow his blessing upon.'*

MILLENNIAL LAWS

SHAKER FOOD AND DRINK

'Shakers' or 'Believers' enjoy the products of nature, with which they are amply supplied, and use all the comforts and conveniences which the fruits of their industry permit. They live not in luxury, but in comfort; not in extravagance but in sufficiency.

THE SHAKER (1871)

above

Hancock

The Round Barn at the Hancock Shaker Village was built to house their cattle in near perfect conditions. The Shakers respected all animals but were never sentimental about them.

Although initially quite restricted, as the Shaker settlements flourished, the diet of the Believers was exceptionally healthy for the times in which they lived. Although there were lean years, in general they enjoyed plentiful supplies of meat, fresh fruit, vegetables and dairy products. In the early days alcohol was an everyday drink, especially cider and apple brandy – this was partly from common usage at the time – and also because water supplies were far from pure. Later on, *The Millennial Laws* (1845) forbade 'ardent spirits' except for medicinal purposes, although wine appears to have been viewed differently! *Pure wines do not intoxicate like alcoholic liquors; they do not demoralize but they have a direct tendency to elevate and improve the moral condition of society.*

A MANUAL OF WINEMAKING

In general it appears that this law was not strictly enforced, except on Sundays, although there are records of apple trees being felled to discourage the production of cider. Some of the injunctions regarding food were on the eccentric side: cucumbers were not to

be eaten unless seasoned with salt or pepper and raw fruit and nuts were only allowed between breakfast and six in the evening.

WHAT HAPPENED TO THE SHAKERS?

Today there is only one surviving Shaker community where a handful of Believers live and work at Sabbathday Lake, Maine. Other settlements, including Hancock, Massachusetts, and Canterbury and Enfield in New Hampshire, and South Union and Pleasant Hill, Kentucky are now museum villages, lovingly restored and tended by enthusiasts of the Shaker way of life.

From the middle of the 19th century there was a slow decline in membership of the Shakers. As life became more comfortable in 'the World', converts were harder to find, and younger members eschewed the hard work, celibacy and strict morality for a freer way of life outside the communities. Provided they openly admitted their attachment, those who fell in love within the settlements were given the community's blessing and released to live

above

Shaker villages

Villages have been carefully restored as heritage sites where visitors can understand more about Shaker life.

in 'the World' with a horse and cart and what amounted to a dowry to help them on their way. For this reason there were few problems with scandalous liaisons.

After the Civil War there was a relaxation of many of the rules, in the hope that this would attract new members. Flower gardens were permitted and listening to music and reading books was no longer forbidden. Women were encouraged to join and enjoy an equality not available elsewhere, which resulted in an imbalance in the membership that was never corrected. As the population of the settlements dwindled, their prosperity diminished and they fell into disrepair. Tyringham in Massachusetts was the first entire community to close down in 1875. By 1947 only 50 Believers remained in three small New England Families.

Mother Ann believed that when there were only as many Shakers left as there are fingers on a child's hand, there would be a second flowering of Shakerism. If that is so then it will have to be the tiny community at Sabbathday Lake that sees a Millennial revival of this remarkable utopian society.

"The garden is *said to be* the index of

the owner's mind. *If this be true,* many who

otherwise might be acquitted, *must* be judged

to possess minds *susceptible* of *much* improvement

in order, usefulness, and beauty'."

The Gardener's Manual

setting

the scene

In choosing a site *for a garden, a spot of even land, slightly inclining to the south or east, and having the full benefit of the sun, is to be preferred. It should be situated near the dwelling, and neatly enclosed.*

THE GARDENER'S MANUAL

WHEN *The Gardener's Manual* was written, the advice on siting a garden was easily followed as most gardeners were cultivating virgin land. Today few of us start gardening with a bare plot that we can transform into the garden of our dreams. Gardens are smaller, more enclosed, and now that we garden mainly for pleasure rather than survival, a favourable aspect is a bonus rather than a necessity. Fortunately for this book, an area of garden that fitted the description given in *The Gardener's Manual* was available for transformation into a Shaker garden. It is situated on a gentle south-eastern slope within a sunny, walled garden and is close to the house.

The advice in *The Gardener's Manual* is useful wherever your garden may be. However, if there is no area of the garden that meets at least some of the criteria, you can save yourself an enormous amount

THE UNPLANTED SHAKER GARDEN

KEY

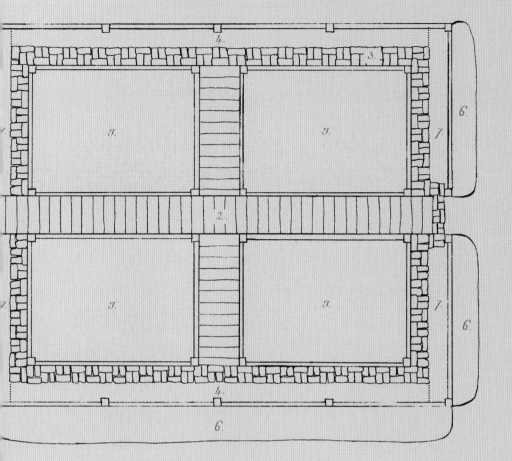

1. Raised beds – 2.4 x 1.8m (8 x 6ft)

2. Board paths – 60cm (2ft) wide

3. Brick paths – 30cm (1ft) wide

4. Narrow borders

5. Picket fence – 7.3 x 5.5m (24 x 18ft)

6. External borders

7. Borders 60cm (2ft) wide

left
Unplanted garden
The Gardener's Manual *described the ideal position and gave details of the plan for the perfect Shaker garden.*

opposite
Shaker scene
The cultivation of a flower garden around the dwelling house would not have been countenanced in the early settlements, but by Victorian times it was seen as a healthy pastime for Shaker women and girls.

of frustration and disappointment by accepting that it is not suitable for a Shaker garden, and instead make more realistic plans for its use. But don't be disheartened – even the most unpromising plot can be 'susceptible of much improvement in order, usefulness, and beauty', and you will find ideas and inspiration for every type of garden within these pages.

The elements of Shaker design – lack of clutter, natural materials and rich (but not gaudy) colours – can be applied to any garden. A thorough tidy is a good start – be ruthless! Throw away the rusty wheelbarrow that is beyond repair, take down the dilapidated trellis that will collapse anyway in the next strong wind, donate the mountain of plastic pots to a good cause and renovate or discard the neglected and broken tools that have accumulated in the shed. There is nothing useful or beautiful about junk.

Look at the hard surfaces. A brick or cobble path has the right feel, but concrete paving may need replacing or disguising. Tackle these projects before you plant. Whether you do it yourself or have professional help it is messy and disruptive and you don't want to worry about your newly planted treasures while it is happening. Now is also the time to erect fencing, create raised beds, paint the shed and generally set the scene. Making a Shaker garden is as much about the preparation as the planting.

Picket Fences

ORIGINALLY A PICKET FENCE *was a practical barrier to prevent livestock and other animals getting into the garden. It can still be used to keep small children and pets at bay, but it can also define an enclosed area or create a change of mood within the garden. The simplest picket fence consists of supporting posts, with cross-rails attached, to which are nailed evenly-spaced, flat-topped wooden pickets or pales as they were also known. In New England and most of America, northern white cedar — with its unsurpassed durability — is the wood that is used for this purpose. In other parts of the world, pine, pressure-treated with preservative can be used instead. The picket fence surrounding my Shaker garden is made from pine.*

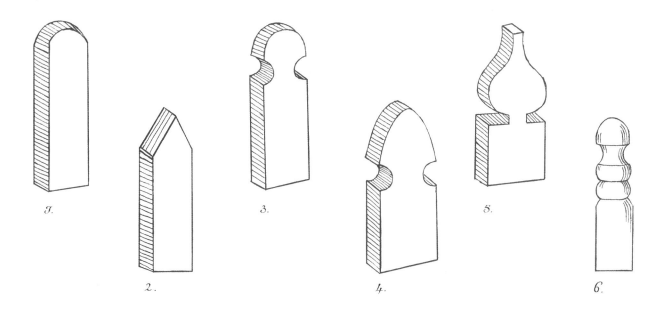

1.

2.

3.

4.

5.

6.

opposite (top left)

Meeting House

A 'candle-flame' picket fence surrounds a Meeting House.

top right

Significant detail

Close-up of the Shaker garden fence.

bottom left

Candle fence detail

This elaborate design was solely for Meeting Houses.

bottom right

Alternative fencing

Post and rail fencing was used for field boundaries.

left

Picket fences

1. Round top picket
2. Nantucket picket
3. Princess Anne picket
4. Queen Anne picket
5. Pendant picket
6. Cambridge spindle

VARIOUS PATTERNS OF PICKET TOPS have traditionally been used for fences in Shaker villages and 'the World'. For example, the picket fences surrounding the Meetinghouses in Shaker settlements are based on the prototype that was erected at New Lebanon. Granite posts hold the wooden pickets above the ground and keep them free from rot. This has ensured that where a settlement survives, the original pickets are still in good condition. Each picket is shaped like a candle topped by a flame, representing the spiritual illumination to be found within the Meetinghouse where the Shakers worshipped.

The Shakers tended to use picket fences sparingly, often using close board fences to confine animals. Post and rail fencing was also used by the Shakers, mainly to fence large areas such as paddocks and fields where livestock was kept, but it is less suitable for gardens as it does not secure the garden effectively from anything but the largest marauders.

Now few of us have the skills, time or equipment to make picket fencing, but fencing manufacturers in most countries will have ready-made lengths available. In America where there is a continuing tradition of using this type of fencing, there is a wide range of heritage patterns available. Elsewhere you may have to make do with flat or pointed tops unless the pickets are specially made.

Before planning the lay-out of your Shaker garden ask your fencing supplier for the measurements of their ready-made lengths of picket fencing. If you plan the perimeter fence based on these measurements you will save money and avoid wastage. Supporting posts should be at least 10cm (4in) square and to ensure a sturdy fence, 45cm (18in) of each post should be fixed below ground level using concrete or tightly-rammed rubble or stones. Painting is not essential for cedar or treated pine, but using one of the colours from the traditional Shaker palette will help underline the theme of the garden.

Paths

THE UTMOST NEATNESS *is conspicuous in their fields, gardens, courtyards, outhouses, and in the very road; not a weed, not a spot of filth, or any nuisance is suffered to exist. Benjamin Silliman on visiting.*

NEW LEBANON IN *1819*

THE SHAKERS' SENSE OF ORDER ensured that each building in a settlement was approached by a neat weatherproof path. Natural materials found in the local area were used to create stone slabbed walks or boarded wooden pathways. In the gardens, the paths between the herb beds that were trodden less frequently – especially during the winter months – were laid to grass and always kept neatly edged and trimmed. As Benjamin Silliman observed on his visit to New Lebanon, the overwhelming impression of the Shaker village was of 'utmost neatness'.

It was not until the late 19th century, when flowerbeds were permitted, that plants softened the severity of the immediate surroundings of the buildings. Surviving Shaker villages have been restored to their original plain condition with the gardens surrounding the houses laid to grass intersected by unadorned stone or boarded pathways. It is interesting to compare their appearance now with archive photographs that show plants encroaching over pathways and clambering up walls.

Unless your taste is for the minimalist, your Shaker garden will probably consist of more than grass and pathways. As I have said before, this is not an exercise in historical accuracy, but the use of sympathetic materials for pathways will help with the overall impression the garden creates. Nowadays real stone slabs are very expensive and although some of the copies do have the appearance of riven stone, their inevitable uniformity reveals their

above

Board path

A wooden pathway leads past the steps to a dwelling house, ensuring that the Shakers could move between buildings without danger of bringing any dirt indoors on their shoes.

origins and they do not weather like real stone. I used old bricks, instead of stone, for some of the smaller pathways in my Shaker garden. These were simply laid upon level soil in a basket weave pattern. At the time of the early Shakers, bricks were handmade and too precious for such a use, whereas local stone was readily available.

In order to prevent perennial weeds establishing themselves in a brick path, first lay a weed-suppressing membrane, cover it with a 5cm (2in) layer of sharp sand and then bed the bricks into the sand. Any annual weeds that self-seed into the sand are easily removed. The main pathways in my garden were made of timber boarding raised above soil level on supporting battens. Once again it is sensible to suppress the growth of weeds by laying a membrane, or you can use thick layers of newspaper, which will be equally effective. The newspaper is laid between the battens and once the timber planks are nailed in place will be invisible. Be sure to use galvanised nails as ordinary nails will rust. Before ordering the wood for your paths, check the standard timber lengths and dimensions that your merchant stocks as these will be the most economical to use. If you draw an accurately measured plan of the paths, it should be possible to order all the wood pre-cut from the timber merchant and save yourself a great deal of work.

left

Brick path

*A brick path can be
made by laying bricks in
a basketweave pattern
on a bed of sand.*

below

Stone path, Hancock

*Where stone was
available it was used to
make the most durable
of all paths which
survive to this day.*

above

**Long wooden path at
Hancock**

*Wood was more readily
available, and easier to
work than stone so it
was used extensively to
make the pathways in
Shaker villages.*

right

Cross section

*This diagram reveals the
structure of a simple
wooden path.*

Raised Beds

THE GARDEN IS ALL MADE *into beds or plats, in size and width suited to the kinds and quantities of vegetables to be grown on them.*

THE GARDENER'S MANUAL

THE SHAKERS FIRST USED PLOUGHS drawn by horses, oxen or even Brothers, and later mechanical ploughs to form the raised beds in their gardens, but these beds also work well in a small garden. They considered that the main benefit of raised beds was the improved drainage, as the hollows or ditches between the beds carried off excess water in excessively wet weather. In other areas of the garden they would plant into ridges or small mounds of soil, both of which are variations of the raised bed.

Modern organic gardeners favour raised beds not only for the improved drainage, but also because they divide the garden into smaller easily workable areas that can be cultivated with a minimum of soil compaction. Once each bed has been dug over, most other work can be carried out from the edge of the bed. In my Shaker garden I keep a sturdy wooden plank at hand, which, when rested on the edges of the raised beds, provides a platform that allows me to work in the centre of the beds without the plank or my feet coming into direct contact with the soil.

right

Raised bed

Raised beds ensure that the paths are for feet and beds are for plants by clearly defining and separating the two areas.

At its simplest, a raised bed can be formed by resting a rectangular wooden frame on top of the soil, or outlining the area with railway sleepers. Initially the bed will be at the same height as the surrounding soil, but over time, as compost and manure are added, the soil level within the frame will increase. If you make your raised beds in this way you need to be sure that the

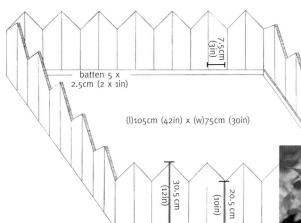

batten 5 x
2.5cm (2 x 1in)

7.5cm
(3in)

(l)105cm (42in) x (w)75cm (30in)

30.5 cm
(12in)

20.5 cm
(10in)

left

Miniature diagram

*This simple framework
can be used to create a
tiny Shaker garden on a
terrace or balcony.*

below

Miniature garden

*Even a garden as tiny
as this can be
surprisingly productive if
it is carefully tended.*

surrounding area is free of persistent perennial weeds such as bindweed and ground elder or they will constantly invade the beds. As the Shaker garden featured in this book is on a slight incline, it was not possible simply to rest the frames on the soil. This would have created a very curious effect with sloping raised beds and level, but stepped, picket fencing. In this instance the raised beds were created by hammering in posts at all four corners, to which were nailed the planks that formed the sides of the beds. Again, galvanised nails were used.

For the two beds on the slightly steeper part of the slope, it was necessary to add a second row of planks to the sides and the lower edges to keep these beds at the same level as the other two.

MINIATURE SHAKER GARDEN

For those without a garden large enough to devote an area to permanent raised beds, a miniature Shaker garden could be the answer. I set this one up in the paved and walled courtyard outside my kitchen. The picket fence is made from ready-made border-edging nailed onto a rectangle of battening 105cm x 75cm (42in x 30in) to hold it rigid. (If you have the skills and equipment you could make it from scratch.)

After painting the fence dark red, the raised bed was three-quarters filled with fine grade composted bark. Each plant was grown in an individual pot, which was concealed by sinking it in the bark. Like all container plants, these needed extra feeding and regular watering, but with this type of attention the miniature garden proved surprisingly fruitful. As plants passed their productive best it was easy to remove them and replace them with something different which had been growing on elsewhere. Over the summer I picked dwarf beans, peppers, tomatoes and ruby chard, as well as enjoying an early display of miniature sunflowers. The sweetcorn was the only plant that did not prove very successful. Like the garden itself, the corn cobs were definitely miniature!

above

Canterbury supports

Sturdy supports are essential for heavy cropping plants like tomatoes or beans.

right

Beanpole

The inherent beauty of the runner bean plant is evident in the way this young shoot has wound its way around the rustic beanpole. Without such sturdy support the plant will be more vulnerable to damage and less productive.

Plant Supports

SHAKER GARDENS WERE PLACES *of 'goodly order', and wherever necessary plant supports formed part of that orderliness. Straight, rustic poles cut from the surrounding woodlands were used as bean poles and frames for heavy-fruiting tomato plants, and twiggy branches gave support to the pea vines.*

UNTIL QUITE RECENTLY every vegetable garden used this type of rustic plant support or bamboo canes, but with the advent of plastics and other modern materials they became less used and harder to obtain unless you had access to your own supply of wood and brush. This is to be regretted because the natural materials have an inherent beauty that plastic will never have. When I started working on my Shaker garden it took me some time to track down a source of rustic poles and pea brush, until it occurred to me that the man who supplied me with firewood may be able to help. Sure enough, as someone who manages an area of woodland, he was able to provide me with wonderfully sturdy beanpoles and armfuls of pea sticks. If you live in an area with less direct access to the countryside you may find these materials somewhat elusive, although with the revival in

left

Beanpoles

Freshly cut bean poles lean against the fence, ready for use.

centre

Plant support

This design of support can be used for tomatoes or for raspberries.

right

Twigs & string

Peasticks are invaluable in the vegetable garden.

interest and appreciation of rustic materials they are sometimes sold at the flower and plant shows that take place early in the year. If not, you may need to enlist the help of a country dwelling friend. Once obtained, the bean poles will last for a number of years, especially if they are stored undercover during the winter.

Surplus bean poles can be arranged in a circle and tied at the top to form a support for climbing rose plants or cut in half to make sturdy sticks to support tomato plants. Pea brush has many uses. Laid loosely across freshly sown soil or newly transplanted seedlings it protects them from birds and stop cats sunbathing (or worse) on the newly raked soil! Short lengths can be pushed into the ground on either side of rows of annual flowers, such as cornflowers and marigolds that have a tendency to sprawl. The sticks will give them sufficient support to remain upright.

Containers

LOOKING AT *archive photographs* *there is little evidence of containers being used in Shaker gardens. In all likelihood they would have been regarded as too ornamental and labour intensive to fit into the Shaker way of life. Today their use is an essential element of most gardens, and their exclusion would limit the usefulness of this book for many readers.*

above

Milk churns

Obsolete agricultural equipment like these old milk churns make sympathetic containers in a Shaker garden. These could be used for plants or better still they would be ideal for storing water or home-made liquid fertiliser or even as a waterproof store for small garden tools, string, packets of seeds etc.

right

Wood tray and pots

Weathered terracotta pots are far more attractive than new ones – leave your new pots outdoors so that they can acquire a similar patina.

below

Various containers

A selection of galvanised metal and enamelled containers which would not look out of place in the Shaker garden.

ONCE AGAIN SIMPLICITY is the key. A mass of pots grouped together would not be in keeping with the Shaker approach, but carefully placed individual containers that are functional as well as decorative would fit in quite well. For instance, where space is limited, a wooden half-barrel can be planted with a courgette (zucchini) plant. In a raised bed, enthusiastic courgette plants can swamp the plants around them – this certainly happened in my Shaker garden where the red sage, basil and aubergines (eggplants) all disappeared under the relentless growth of the courgettes and I had to resort to trimming off some of the leaves to save their companions. Any plant of invasive character could be confined to a container. Mint and lemon balm come to mind, and growing strawberries in a barrel is practical and attractive as well as making them easy to net against marauding birds.

The choice of containers is important. They should be made of a material that will blend well with the rest of the Shaker garden – natural wood, or wood that has been stained or painted in Shaker colours will fit in harmoniously as will weathered terracotta and painted or galvanised tin. If you live in a cold climate zone where many plants need to be brought under cover for the winter, it may make sense to grow the plants in polythene pots and then slip them inside the more appropriate containers when they are in the Shaker garden. Come the winter the plants can be brought under cover and the containers can be left where they are or stored until the spring.

MAKING THE WOODEN SEED TRAYS

**Materials &
Equipment**

*If you are planning to
make a number of trays,
you could ask your timber
merchant to pre-cut the
timber for you. For each
seed tray you will need
the following:*

2 side-pieces –
38 x 5cm (15 x 2in) x
12mm ('/2in)

2 end-pieces – 22 x 5cm
(8¹/2in x 2in) x 12mm ('/2in)

2 base planks – 37 x 10cm
(14¹/2in x 4in) x 12mm ('/2in)

25mm (1in) galvanised
tacks

water-based preservative

wood stain and brush
(optional)

tenon saw
(if cutting your own timber)

hammer

Method

1. Join side-pieces to end-pieces using two tacks
at each corner to form a rectangle.

2. Place the two base planks on the rectangle and
hammer into position using two tacks at each end
of each plank.

3. Paint the finished seed tray with two coats of
preservative wood stain.

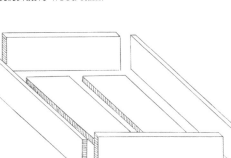

(l)38cm (15in) x (h)5cm (2in) x (w)22cm (8¹/2in)

WOODEN SEED TRAYS

Since the advent of plastics, few of us use wooden seed trays any more. Plastic trays are lighter, cheaper and easier
to clean, but while they are eminently practical, there is little beauty in their utility. However the Shakers would
not have dismissed such an innovation, although they may have refined it, and there are times when plastic seed
trays are right for the job. Nonetheless a few wooden seed trays will come in useful in the Shaker garden. They
can be used as outer sleeves for flimsy plastic trays and as a container to display groups of potted plants.

above

Wooden seed trays
*Unlike plastic seedtrays
wooden trays are
attractive objects and if
they are cleaned and
stored during the winter
they will last years.*

The Shed

WITH MUCH OF THE *Shakers' daily activity linked to horticulture and agriculture their settlements included many buildings that supported these activities. As well as having barns and outbuildings to house meticulously orderly tools, machinery and equipment, there were sheds for drying, sorting and packing herbs; rooms where herbs were processed into pills, tinctures and patent medicines and other areas devoted to drying, cleaning and packaging seeds, as well as winter stores for fruit and vegetables. Everything had its pre-ordained place, and such was the discipline and orderliness of the communities that one would always know with certainty where an item could be found.*

FOR MOST OF US a single shed must suffice in a modern Shaker garden – and lacking the external discipline and moral authority that guided all aspects of the Shaker way of life, orderliness is not always the priority it might be. Personally I am sporadically tidy and – once the task has been faced – I reap both pleasure and benefit from my efforts. During the year in which I have cultivated the Shaker garden I have worked hard at creating order behind the scenes as well as in the garden itself. Throughout this time I have frequently observed to myself, and to others, that any task is simpler if everything you need is accessible and ready-for-use.

Take a long, hard look at your shed. Is the floor cluttered with a web of entangled tools, string, boxes and things that might be useful? Is the work bench clear or covered with empty seed packets, old labels, pots of dry soil and worn out gloves? Choose a fine day and take everything outside. Sweep out the shed, including brushing down the shelves and bench and clean the window. Dust and cobwebs significantly cut down on the light entering a shed making it hard to see where things are and also adversely affecting the growth of any seedlings or plants that may be on the workbench.

With the shed clean and empty you can consider how to organise it so that it stays that way for as long as possible. There is no point in putting something that you use frequently at the back of the shed – make it easily accessible and you are much more likely to put it back there after use. If there is wall space, use it to

above

Storage

Keeping a work place tidy is much easier if you have sufficient storage containers, boxes and baskets to allow you to store different items separately. It cuts down on muddle and encourages tidiness.

top left

Tidy tools

A wooden barrel in the corner keeps large tools orderly and accessible.

top right

Broom and dustpan

A dustpan and brush next to the door encourages tidy habits.

opposite

Hancock shed

Working buildings at Shaker villages were painted in dark colours – this shed in the herb garden at the Hancock Shaker village is painted a deep red – it would look good in a modern Shaker garden.

hang tools. Mark the position of each by outlining it with a permanent marker – that way everyone will know where that tool belongs. Hang plastic or metal funnels from hooks above the workbench and use each one for different types of twine and string, with the ends threaded through the funnel ends. Next to the string, have a pair of scissors attached to a length of chain that is securely attached to the shed wall (string doesn't work – someone will cut it and liberate the scissors).

A hanging basket or other wire basket suspended from the ceiling next to the door is a good place to keep gardening gloves.

They are near-at-hand and the air circulation stops them going mouldy. Decant bags of potting compost, loam etc. into lidded dustbins to stand under the workbench or just outside the shed door with smaller bins for sharp sand, gravel etc. The shed will be far easier to keep tidy without all those plastic sacks spilling their contents each time you use them. Store seeds in a lidded box, preferably an airtight one. Check the seeds at the end of the growing season, and discard any that are out of date. The shed is the engine room of the garden and when kept in good order will help keep the garden in similar good order.

SEED PACKETS

The following seeds are selected with peculiar care, being the choicest kinds of the different varieties; and as such they will recommend themselves. They will be sold on the most reasonable terms by the pound, or put up in small papers for retailing, to suit the convenience of the customer.

A CATALOGUE OF GARDEN SEEDS RAISED BY THE UNITED SOCIETY OF SHAKERS, MOUNT LEBANON, COLUMBIA COUNTY, NEW YORK.

Before the Shakers introduced the seed packet, all seed was sold by the pound – which was good for farmers, but too expensive and far more than was needed for the domestic gardener who only needed sufficient to grow food for the family. The Shakers revolutionised the selling of seed by packaging the seeds in 'small papers' and guaranteeing the purity and freshness of their products. Initially the seed packets were modest affairs made from plain paper, but later on, as they competed with other seed purveyors from 'the World' their packets became both colourful and very decorative.

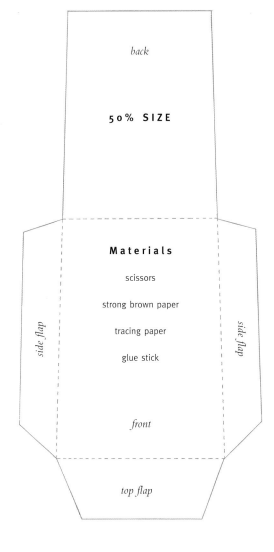

back

50% SIZE

Materials

scissors

strong brown paper

tracing paper

glue stick

side flap

side flap

front

top flap

MAKING SEED PACKETS

The simplicity of these seed packets is reminiscent of the early style of packaging used by the Shakers.

Method

1. Take a tracing of the packet design (left), double its size using a photocopier, and transfer it onto the brown paper.

2. Cut out as many seed packets as you require.

3. Fold the packet along the fold line between the front and back.

4. Fold along the side flaps between the front and sides and glue in place.

5. Fold top flap over.

6. Once the packet is filled the top flap can be tucked inside the packet or closed with glue.

opposite

Shaker lettering

Shaker seeds were renowned for their quality and their distinctive packaging was instantly recognisable – before the Shakers all seed was sold in bulk.

below left

Seed packets

Home-made seed packets may not have the pretty pictures of those available commercially but they won't have a hefty price tag either!

centre

Seed store

Before seed packets were readily available to the gardener, seeds would sometimes be kept in little interlocking wooden boxes.

below right

Seeds

Once you have collected your own seed, don't forget to sow them next year – some seeds only remain viable for a season or two, especially when they aren't hermetically sealed like the commercial varieties.

top row (left to right)
Garden accessories

Although they each have an intrinsic beauty all these objects are primarily functional so their use is appropriate within a Shaker garden.

Accessories

THE IDEA OF ACCESSORIES *is not one that sits entirely happily within the framework of the Shaker philosophy, denoting as it does unnecessary decorative touches. However, if you keep in mind the phrase 'useful beauty' when choosing accessories for your modern Shaker garden, you will stay true to the essence of their beliefs. In other words the functional objects in the garden should have a beauty and the beautiful objects should have a function.*

below
Barrow

Shaker artefacts such as this barrow are far too valuable to use in the garden, but well-made, light-weight, modern equivalents are available

I NEEDED FEW ACCESSORIES within my Shaker garden, but those I did incorporate I chose with care. Bamboo plant cloches were perfect for strawberries – allowing good air circulation around the fruit, but preventing marauding birds from feasting on the berries. With the Shaker talent for basket-making their use was entirely appropriate, although mine were in fact made in China.

Instead of a conventional water-butt, I used an antique 'dolly' tub. These galvanised metal tubs were used for washing clothes in the days before washing machines. Stood at the end of one of the paths, the tub is topped up by hose when routine watering takes place and in between I use water from the tub when a plant needs a boost or when transplanting young plants or watering freshly sown seeds.

The Shakers were great bee-keepers and I would love to have had a hive in the garden, but I have neither the knowledge nor the confidence to manage one. Also the garden is really too small for us to co-exist without incident, so I found a garden store built in the shape of a traditional beehive. My shed is in another part of the garden and this small store has proved very useful. I keep a waterproof coat in it to protect me from sudden downpours, a change of footwear, a hat and sunscreen for sunny days, use it to store hand tools and gardening gloves and keep seeds handy for successional sowing. The 'hive' looks perfectly at home in the Shaker garden and has more than proved its usefulness.

top row (left to right)

Goodly order

*A beehive in the Shaker
garden opens to reveal
that it is actually a
storage bin containing
wellington boots, a straw
hat and a ball of string.
Baskets provide useful
storage in the shed.*

centre (left to right)

Peg rail storage

*Looking at the rows of
straw hats and watering
cans suspended from peg
rails at the Hancock
Shaker Village, one can
imagine each gardener
donning a hat and
taking a can as he went
to work in the garden
each day.
Many Shaker baskets
were made with handles
by which they could be
hung from pegs.*

bottom (left to right)

Shaker design

*Everything the Shakers
used in their villages –
from cart to colander –
was designed and made
in their workshops
following the principle of
'beauty through utility'*

BIRDHOUSES

The Shakers were respectful of all natural life but there was little room in their lives for sentiment. They were instructed that 'no beasts, birds, fowls, or fishes may be kept merely for the sake of show or fancy'. Nonetheless beneficial wild birds would have been welcomed to their gardens as pollinators and insect eaters.

below

Hanging birdhouse

High up in an apple tree, this birdhouse will be hidden from predators when the leaves unfurl.

right

Nesting box

Fashioned from an old crate, this birdhouse has lettering reminiscent of that used in Shaker advertisements of the 1800s.

Today we understand how important it is to provide havens for these birds as our gardens have become more welcoming than many of their traditional habitats in the countryside. Birdhouses in the Shaker garden should reflect the architecture and materials used in their settlements, and in keeping with the Shaker philosophy of useful beauty, should be positioned where they are likely to be used by birds, rather than purely as decorative accessories.

SHINGLE-ROOFED BIRDHOUSE

An old wooden crate with attractive lettering was used to make this rustic birdhouse, with a handgrip forming the entrance. The shingle roof is made from the sides and base of a discarded vegetable box. The ledge at the base of the front panel was part of the original crate and was left in place because the lettering contributed to the overall effect. The crate was bought in a junk shop, but if you find it difficult to locate a similar one, you could use plain timber. The dimensions of the birdhouse were largely dictated by the size of the crate and, providing the proportions are the same, it is best to remain flexible when making your own.

MAKING THE SHINGLE-ROOFED BIRDHOUSE

Materials & Equipment

wooden crate –
approximately 45 x 30cm
(18 x 12in)

vegetable box – similar
proportions

saw

hammer

3cm (1¼in) tacks

wood glue

sandpaper

paintbrush

water-based satin varnish

burnt umber acrylic paint

below

Roof shingles

*Shingles made from the
wood of a vegetable box.*

Method

1. Carefully dismantle the wooden crate into its component parts and cut as follows:

- *front and back – 15.5 x 16.5cm (6¼ x 6½in)*
  – use a piece of timber with a handgrip for the front;
- *side panels – 13 x 16.5cm (5¼ x 6½in);*
- *roof apex x 2 – 12cm high x 16.5cm wide (4¼ x 6.5in);*
- *baseboard 20 x 20cm (8in x 8in) – it may be necessary to join two pieces of timber.*

2. Cut the perch from a spare piece of timber and sand smooth. Knock two tacks through from the back of the front panel, just below the entrance. Apply glue to the back of the perch and gently tap into position over the tacks.

3. Glue and tack the front, sides and back together to form a rectangle. Turn the rectangle upside down and tack the baseboard in position.

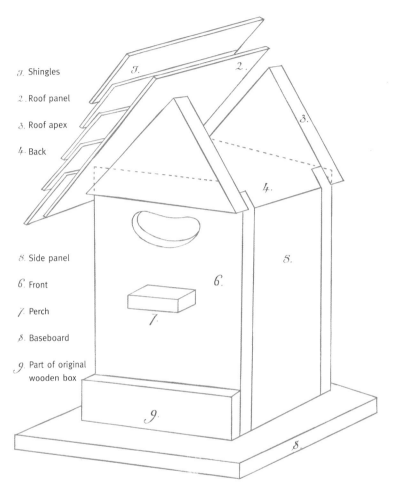

1. Shingles
2. Roof panel
3. Roof apex
4. Back
5. Side panel
6. Front
7. Perch
8. Baseboard
9. Part of original wooden box

4. Glue and tack the apex to the front panel – there should be a 2.5cm (1in) overlap. Use the saw to trim off the top corners of the front panel parallel with the apex so that they do not protrude. Repeat step 4 for the back panel.

5. Dismantle the vegetable box and use the largest pieces to cut two rectangles to form the roof of the birdhouse. Glue and tack in place ensuring that they fit tight together along the ridge.

6. Cut shingles 6cm (2⅜in) deep from the remainder of the vegetable box and, starting at the bottom edge of each pitch, glue the shingles into place, overlapping one another up to the ridge.

7. Sand rough edges, then paint the body of the birdhouse with satin varnish. Mix a small quantity of burnt umber acrylic paint with satin varnish and paint the shingles to age the wood and blend it with the rest of the birdhouse.

Tools

NO ONE SHOULD TAKE TOOLS, *belonging in charge of others, without obtaining liberty for the same. When any one borrows a tool, it should be immediately returned, without injury, if possible, and if injured, should be made known by the borrower to the lender.*

THE MILLENNIAL LAWS *(1845)*

top left

Can handle

Old, galvanised watering cans have a simple, practical beauty – perfect for the Shaker garden.

centre

Plant labels

Fibre pots and wooden labels are ready in the potting shed for spring seed sowing.

IN *THE GARDENERS MANUAL* THE SHAKERS listed the tools required for the management of a garden as follows: '*a plough, harrow, rake, hoes, spade, shovel, dung-fork, watering pot, transplanting-trowel, a long and strong line, or cord, and a wooden roller 18 inches in diameter and 4 feet long. Perhaps bean poles, pea brush, a quantity of garden stakes and twine, might with propriety be added to the list. These are generally sufficient – although we are aware that others will at times be wanted, as the crow-bar in setting the bean poles, the pruning knife, shears, or sickle in trimming and gathering the crops at times.*'

This list is as relevant today as it was then with the exception of the plough, harrow and wooden roller, which related to large scale gardening and given a few minor adjustments such as exchanging the dung-fork for an ordinary fork and the sickle for a strimmer. What place, you may wonder, would a strimmer have in a Shaker garden? The Shakers were

above

Pea brush

*A line of twiggy sticks
are positioned to support
soon-to-emerge pea
plants. A ball of twine
and two bamboo canes
make a simple guideline.*

never averse to innovation – after all it was they who invented the first seed-drill. They considered that more efficient tools allowed them to do a better job, although they never thought of them as 'labour-saving', which was not a concept that had any place in Shaker life. Time freed from one task was immediately allocated to another.

The Shakers were as disciplined in their gardens as they were in the rest of their lives and the care and maintenance of tools was of primary importance. These tools were expected to last a lifetime, or even longer. In our modern throw-away society this is a lesson we could well learn. Buying good quality tools is wasted money if they are left to rust where they were last used. Develop the habit of cleaning and putting tools away when you are finished in the garden each day, and they will reward you with long and reliable service.

opposite right

Wooden spade handle

*Years of use have worn
smooth the wood and
metalwork of a spade.*

above

Hand tools

Hand tools stand ready for use in a wire basket which can be taken out into the garden.

right

Antique tools

Tools should always be thoroughly cleaned before they are put away, and if they are stored where they are easily accessible it will be much easier to keep them tidy and in good condition. These old tools have a lovely patina to them, but they do need to be carefully maintained. The Shakers would have gratefully embraced modern easy-care stainless steel tools which are just as efficient, lighter and more durable.

It is still possible to buy wonderful old garden tools at quite reasonable prices. Generally 'Ladies' forks and spades are better proportioned for the contemporary gardener – the full-size implements are often extremely heavy and unwieldy. There is a pleasure in handling these tools with their tines and blades that have been partially worn away through years of use. It shows that they have proved to be the right tool for the job, unlike many of the gimmicky 'revolutionary' tools that are advertised in the gardening press today. The hand tools, the forks and trowels, with their handles worn smooth by earlier gardeners, have a strength to them that is seldom found in their modern counterparts.

Old galvanised watering cans come in all shapes and sizes, although the larger ones should be avoided as they can be extremely heavy when full of water. I have a favourite one-gallon can that I use in the Shaker garden. It is stood next to the 'dolly' tub, so that I can dip it into the tub and water thirsty plants without always resorting to the hose. In winter galvanised cans should be brought into the shed or

top row (left to right)

Brushes

A stiff hand brush is invaluable for brushing out pots and seed trays, while a soft brush will keep compost in a tidy heap when you are potting up plants.

Wooden box

A compartmented wooden box with a carrying handle proved to be useful in the Shaker garden ensuring that tools and gloves were close to hand.

Secateurs

Good quality, sharp secateurs are essential equipment in the garden. Not only do they cut more easily, but they cut more cleanly as well, so that there is less likelihood of the plant being damaged by poor pruning.

stored upside down so that water does not freeze in them and cause damage.

One should not be too carried away with nostalgia however. The Shakers would certainly have used modern materials to make well-designed and efficient implements. Modern tools are often lighter, and may be easier to use and care for than the old-fashioned, handmade tools with which the Shakers were familiar.

To keep tools in good condition, it is essential that they are properly cleaned after use. In dry conditions they need only be brushed and wiped down with an oily cloth; in damp or wet conditions tools should be brushed, washed to remove any soil that adheres to them and then dried before wiping down. An alternative to an oily cloth is a bucket filled with sand to which oil has been added. After preliminary cleaning, plunge tools into the oily sand before returning them to their allotted place. Wooden handles should be wiped regularly with an oily rag or the wood will dry and split. Tools that have blades – spades, hoes, secateurs – should be sharpened annually.

Paints

IN EARLY SHAKER VILLAGES *the colour a building was painted related to its function. White paint, symbolic of purity, was reserved for spiritual buildings.* The Millennial Laws *(1845) required that buildings that lined streets should be 'of a lightish hue', while barns and other buildings away from the road should be darker – red, brown or 'lead colour'. Workbuildings were traditionally painted red, tan or yellow.*

left

Regular maintenance

Wooden buildings look good all year but need painted regularly or they lose the well-cared-for appearance that is characteristic of the Shakers' buildings.

PAINT WAS SEEN PRIMARILY as a protective coating for the building. In some ways, with the exception of the white-painted Meeting houses, the colour was incidental, although given the requirement for control and uniformity which characterised the Shaker way of life, it was inevitable that *The Millennial Laws* (1845) would devise rules for what colours could be used on which buildings. This ensured that there was no temptation to 'decorate' buildings whose architecture was similarly unadorned. Visitors from 'the World', used to more variety and embellishment in their buildings, found the Shaker buildings overlarge and dreadfully dull. When Charles Dickens visited New Lebanon in 1842 he was unimpressed and described them as no better than English factories and barns.

Paints were not mass-manufactured at the time, so like everyone else, the Shakers made their own paints. Some of their paint recipes can be found in an 1848-1849 handwritten book *Receipt Book Concerning Paints, Stains, Cements, Dyes, Inks & c.,*

which is inscribed 'Rosetta Hendrickson A present from Eld. Austin'. From this book it is clear that the Shakers generally used materials that were inexpensive and readily available such as linseed oil or poppy seed oil, combined with traditional mineral pigments such as yellow ochre, raw sienna and iron oxide red. The more expensive materials such as verdigris, gum shellac and Chinese vermilion were reserved for furniture rather than external use. The natural pigments created a generally muted palette that was later superseded by the clear colours of chemical dyes, but is appreciated now for its subtlety and appropriateness when used on period architecture.

There would have been little use of paint in the Shaker gardens of the past – although the fences that can be seen in archive photographs and those in surviving Shaker communities today all seem to be painted white. This is likely to be a practice that was adopted with the advent of mass-manufactured paints. Careful examination of some late 19th century photos reveals that areas in front of Dwellings and Meeting houses were painted white, but the sides and backs were left unpainted.

opposite (top left)

Shaker colours

Shaker garden accessories were painted using traditional Shaker colours.

opposite (top right)

Decorative style

An unusually decorative porch is painted the same colour as the rest of the house.

opposite

Warm colour

The warm colour of the paintwork softens the stark simplicity of the building.

In recent years there has been a proliferation of paint ranges based on historic recipes and colours, including milk paints and traditional linseed oil based formulations like those that were used by the Shakers. These paints were the forerunners of the gloss and emulsion paints which we use today. With names like 'Covered Bridge Red', 'Corner Cupboard Blue' and 'Linen Cupboard White', the modern equivalents are guaranteed to appeal to those who would like to recapture the colours of an earlier time. Technological advances ensure that these paints are far more stable than they were in the past.

I chose 'Corner Cupboard Blue' for the picket fence that surrounds the Shaker garden. Blue is a wonderful colour to use in the garden as it alters in different lights. At dawn and dusk it intensifies, drawing the eye irresistibly. On sunny days it harmonises softly with the surrounding plants and on dreary days it provides a welcome splash of colour. There are plenty of other colours to choose from if blue does not appeal to you or does not fit comfortably into the surrounding area.

The little fence surrounding the miniature Shaker garden was painted 'Covered Bridge Red' to complement the colours in a courtyard garden that was planted with predominantly red, yellow and orange plants. Within the range of appropriate colours, the choice you make is just as much about personal taste as it is about the Shaker palette. If you find yourself totally bemused you can always play safe and paint your fence white, preferably an off-white, which is less stark than pure white.

The picket fence was the only fixed part of the Shaker garden that was painted. The rest of the wood – the paths and the frames for the raised beds – were left to weather naturally. Trugs, seed trays and a stool were painted in another shade of blue, a soft grey-green and a putty colour. Because all these colours have the same opaque, flat finish they look wonderful alongside one another and they add depth and richness to the contours of the wood. As we are frequently warned, colour charts are seldom accurate, so you would be well-advised to try out your chosen colours on a small area before you make a final decision, and remember that colours look quite different according to how the light falls on them.

opposite
(top to bottom)
Traditional colours
The palette of colours used to paint Shaker buildings is derived from the natural pigments which were available at the time. This is why many of the colours have an earthy, muted and opaque quality to them. The buildings within a Shaker settlement may have been painted very different colours, but because they were tonally similar they blended together harmoniously.

left
Dark red shed
The deep red of this shed at the Hancock Shaker Village is a colour which was much used around New England, not just in the Shaker communities. It is a colour that was traditionally used to paint barns and also the covered bridges of the region. As it ages it weathers to a soft pinky-brown; whether freshly painted or gently aged it is a colour which always look good in the landscape.

The Shakers

"*looked* upon the soil as something to be

redeemed from *rugged* barrenness into

smiling fertility and beauty "

Hepworth Dixon in 'New America' *1867*

the soil

'... deep, dry, light, and rich,

are the essential requisites of a good garden soil;

and if not so naturally, it should be made so by

art. If wet, draining should be resorted to; if too

shallow, deep ploughing; if poor, manuring; if

stony, they should be got off; and thus should

every impediment and obstruction to a good sweet

soil, be reversed or removed, by industry and art.'

THE GARDENER'S MANUAL

THE SHAKERS UNDERSTOOD that to grow healthy and productive plants it was essential to have healthy and productive soil. They knew that with hard work they could transform the most unpromising soil into gardens of 'smiling fertility', which would become more fertile as the years went by. In the early years of each community, the gardeners worked as pioneers clearing scrubland to establish their gardens. During its first season the newly cleared land was planted with a crop of potatoes or other root vegetables to help clean the soil and prepare it for general cultivation. This is a practice that is still carried out today to help bring grassland weeds and pests under control on freshly cultivated land. A single crop is easier to manage – the whole plot can be weeded, earthed-up or cleared at the same time. You are unlikely to get a bumper crop, but the produce is a side-product of this beneficial process.

At the end of the first season, or in the early spring of the following year, the soil was thoroughly manured and then cultivated. Regular manuring was part of the routine in Shaker gardens. Poor soils were heavily manured and even fertile soils were given a light dressing to ensure continuing fertility. It was, in fact, compost rather than pure manure that

the Shakers used on their gardens, made to a specific recipe containing minerals, vegetable matter and farmyard manure.

In treating the soil in this way the Shakers were building and improving its natural fertility and ensuring that the land remained healthy and productive for future generations. This is traditional good husbandry, which is also the basis of modern organic gardening. It was only in the 20th century that chemical fertilisers, weedkillers and pesticides encouraged gardeners to take another approach. Short-term gain was all – bigger, better crops, little or no insect damage and weed-free gardens. It is becoming increasingly apparent that there is a price to pay for this type of horticulture and agriculture which, at its most extreme, reduces the soil to an inert medium from which all life has been removed before pumping it full of a cocktail of artificial substances. The Shakers understood that they were the guardians of the soil's fertility and I would encourage modern gardeners to follow their example.

above

Shaker soil

The Shakers were extraordinarily productive gardeners using every inch of their land to grow crops in a soil which progressively got better as they improved it with compost, careful cultivation and good management.

Soil Types

AS SOMEONE WHO HAS SPENT *most of my gardening life trying to improve and enliven heavy clay soils, one of the greatest joys of cultivating the Shaker garden has been working with a light, fertile, sandy soil; but not everyone will be as fortunate and you may find that you will need to enhance your soil before you can achieve satisfactory results.*

IN ORDER TO IMPROVE your soil, you will need to understand it. The easiest, and one of the best ways to do this is to pick up a handful of soil and rub it between your fingers. If it feels gritty it contains sand; clay soil is sticky; silt soil is smooth and silky feeling; peaty soil is black and moist; and chalk soil is pale, dry and crumbly.

Gritty or sandy soil is made up of coarse particles and is light, free draining and well-aerated, which means that the conditions are good for the microscopic organisms which are essential for soil vitality. It can be lacking in humus, so it is essential to incorporate plenty in the form of compost, well-rotted manure and other organic matter, to give the soil 'body' and improve moisture retention during dry weather. Because it is free-draining this type of soil can be cultivated in most conditions without causing compaction.

Clay or silt soils are made up of very fine particles that stick together excluding air and making it difficult for micro-organisms to survive. During dry weather this type of soil tends to harden and form a rock-like crust on the surface. In wet weather it becomes sticky and unmanageable and is impossible to cultivate. In my experience this type of soil, before improvement, is workable for a few weeks at the beginning and end of the season, but the rest of time is best left alone or you are likely to cause further damage to the soil structure. To improve clay or silt soils you need to incorporate air and work in plenty of organic matter, preferably something quite coarse, like compost, which will improve the texture of the soil.

Peaty soil is naturally rich, comprised as it is of decomposed vegetable matter. If you have this type of soil you will need to do little to improve its structure or fertility, both of which are excellent. However, because it is very acid it will be necessary to add lime regularly. Peat soils should not be allowed to dry out completely in hot weather as they then find it difficult to re-absorb water. Regular light watering, or the use of moisture retaining mulches is recommended in these conditions.

Chalk soil tends to be full of stones and flints. With its pale colouring it looks impoverished and as it is very free-draining, this does mean that it doesn't hold water or nutrients effectively. Chalk soils are extremely alkaline and can be quite shallow, with rock just below the surface. This is a difficult soil as many plants will not tolerate these conditions. A chalk soil needs the addition of copious amounts of organic matter, particularly acid materials, such as grass cuttings or composted bark that will help counteract the alkalinity of the soil.

opposite

Hancock Shaker soil

Shaker gardens were frequently carved out from virgin land which had to be cleared of vegetation and large rocks and boulders before it could be cultivated. Even then it was frequently of poor quality and early crops were disappointing. Years of careful management transformed these unpromising fields into the fertile gardens of today.

right

A fine tilth

The Shakers knew that a good seed bed was essential before any seed could be sown. They prepared the soil meticulously, always bearing in mind the needs of the seeds to be sown – the finer the seed the finer the tilth that was required. As the Parable of the Sower taught them they endeavoured always to sow on good ground and let nothing fall upon stony soil or by the wayside.

Cultivating

EXPERIENCE HAS PROVED *that the crop will be improved by good cultivation, both in quantity and quality, more than in proportion to the additional expense incurred, till perfection is attained, where, of course, improvement must stop.*

THE GARDENER'S MANUAL

THE SHAKERS STROVE towards perfection in everything that they did, including cultivating the land. Perfection is a touch ambitious – and unrealistic – but it is undoubtedly true that well-cultivated land will yield far more than an inhospitable and poorly-prepared patch.

DIGGING

Digging the soil is the first step. Deep digging with a spade will quickly reveal many of the virtues and vices of a particular garden. My Shaker garden proved to be easy going with its light, sandy soil and very few stones, but it did have some difficult perennial weeds that needed to be carefully removed. On larger pieces of land it can be tempting to use a mechanical cultivator, but do be cautious if perennial weeds are present. This type of machine will cut up weed roots and multiply the problem rather than solving it. Heavy soils are best dug over in the autumn (fall) at a time when the soil is neither rock-hard nor waterlogged. Leave the surface rough over winter as this will assist drainage and allow frost to work its way into as much of the soil as possible.

RAKING

The next thing is to rake the beds; which on those designed for fine seeds or those to be sown in drills, should be thoroughly and finely done. On those designed for planting beans, squashes & c., you need not be so particular.

THE GARDENER'S MANUAL

Once again the Shakers advice is sound, and there is a practical latitude in permitting the gardener to be less particular with preparing the tilth for larger seeds such as beans and squashes. This is good common sense. Although the Shakers were firm believers in the work ethic, they did not believe in unnecessary work. The raking of light soils is quickly achieved, but once again heavy soil will prove more recalcitrant. Do not attempt to rake it when wet – wait for the right conditions and it will work down nicely without smearing or sticking to the rake.

HOEING

There are three manners of hoeing necessary to be made use of in the garden, which may be distinguished by the names of 1st, flat hoeing, 2nd, digging, and 3rd, hilling. The first is made use of merely to kill the weeds; the second to promote the growth of the plants, by mellowing the soil; and the third to support and nourish some plants in their more advanced stages, by drawing the earth up around their stems, or stalks.

THE GARDENER'S MANUAL

The Shakers were enthusiastic in their use of the hoe. They believed that the soil should be worked constantly to prevent weeds and assist aeration. As they did not generally like the idea of mulches, which they considered untidy, regular hoeing was essential for weed control. The modern gardener is more kindly disposed towards mulches, a practical and efficient method of suppressing weeds around established plants, but it is still true that regular hoeing will control weeds in preparation for mulching later on.

Growing   ONE FOR THE SHAKERS, *one for the crows and one for the thieves.*

SOWING, THINNING & TRANSPLANTING

Stretch a line from end to end, over your bed, for a guide in drilling, then with the corner of your hoe, a pointed stick, or an instrument made for the purpose, drill shallow furrows across the bed from north to south, in depth and distance apart, accommodated to the kinds of seeds which you wish to sow.

THE GARDENER'S MANUAL

As seed merchants, it was in the interest of the Shakers to give their customers information on how to grow seeds successfully. A happy customer will come back for more. The first *Gardener's Manual* was published in 1836 and sold 16,000 copies, to be followed by the expanded 1843 version which has been the source of much wisdom for this book. The majority of the advice in the Manual is good common-sense and is as understandable today as it was then. There is no need to interpret the instructions given above for sowing seeds, except to say that once the seeds have been sown thinly in the drill, the soil should be raked over, gently tamped down with the back of the rake and then watered.

SOAKING SEEDS

In a very dry season, or when you happen to be very late in stocking your garden, soaking the seed a few hours, in luke-warm water, will be beneficial to some kinds; but generally, if sown in proper season, all good seeds will germinate quite as well without soaking, and to seeds of the cabbage kind, it is a positive injury.

THE GARDENER'S MANUAL

The Shakers recognised that not all gardeners were as efficient and organised as they were, so this information about soaking seeds would have been a godsend for those late getting started, and,

from a commercial point of view, it presumably extended the seed-selling season! When seeds are sown under cover in pots or trays it often pays to pre-soak them as this will shorten the length of time they will need to take up space in the greenhouse or cold frame.

THINNING

Thinning may be performed at twice, the first time as soon as the plants are fairly in sight, the second after they are large enough to show which will make thrifty plants. As the quality of the crop, as well as the quantity, frequently depends very much upon this branch of cultivation, it is important that it be seasonably and faithfully performed. Leaving plants too thick is a prevalent error, and one to which gardeners are very liable.

THE GARDENER'S MANUAL

TRANSPLANTING

A prevalent, but erroneous opinion concerning transplanting is, that it should be done just before a shower, in order to succeed well; but experience has shown that a day or two after, when the ground has become dry enough to work again, in the evening, is a preferable time, and perhaps with the exception of cloudy weather, is the best that can be selected. The ground should be prepared as directed for sowing, the plants should be taken up with as much dirt as possible adhering to them, which will be promoted by watering plentifully, before taking them up. A hole deep enough for the roots to enter at full length, should be made, the plants set upright, and fine fresh earth pressed against the roots on all sides. Tender plants will sometimes need watering and shading a day or two after transplanting.

THE GARDENER'S MANUAL *(1843)*

top row

Sowing seeds

When sowing seeds the general rule is that the bigger the seeds the thicker the covering of soil should be. Most small seeds need only have a light covering of sieved soil for them to germinate. Always label as you sow.

centre left

Potting on

Pot on seedlings before they get too large. Seed compost contains few nutrients and they will soon need a richer soil.

centre right

Taking cuttings

Most cuttings will root in sharp sand.

bottom left

Potting compost

Most commercially produced potting composts contain sufficient nutrients to last six weeks, which will be fine for plants which are then planted in the garden. If there is a delay, liquid feed regularly to keep the plants growing strongly.

bottom right

Pricking out

Ideally seedlings should be pricked out once they have formed their first set of proper leaves, then watered gently after they are transplanted. They can be watered more thoroughly once they have perked up. Always hold the seedling by its leaves, not its stem.

MAKING A SOIL TAMPER

Materials & Equipment	Method
	1. Sandpaper any rough areas of the handle and round off one end.
20cm (8in) length of broom handle	**2.** Sandpaper the piece of timber, rounding off all the corners.
20cm (8in) length of 5 x 2cm (2in x ¾in) timber	**3.** Mark the centre point of the timber and drill a hole the correct size for the screw you are using.
5cm (2in) brass screw	**4.** Insert the screw and position the handle so that the screw will penetrate it centrally.
medium sandpaper	**5.** Tighten the screw.
electric drill	
screwdriver	

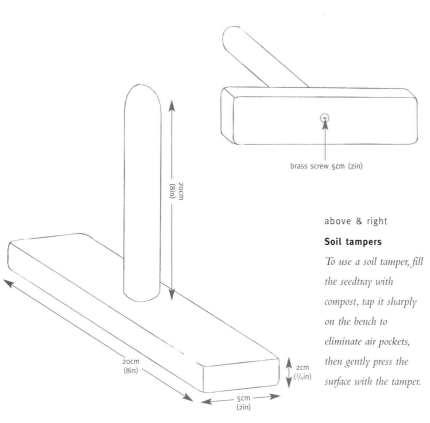

brass screw 5cm (2in)

20cm (8in)

20cm (8in)

2cm (¾in)

5cm (2in)

above & right

Soil tampers

To use a soil tamper, fill the seedtray with compost, tap it sharply on the bench to eliminate air pockets, then gently press the surface with the tamper.

Weeds

AH! HERE ARE OUR *old friends*
again. But we cannot afford to keep them though there is a world
of beauty in each. Like all living things, they seek to perpetuate
their kind, and will deposit countless thousands of their minute
seeds to make sure a future crop. Faithful constant hoeing only will
prevent their being in the ascendant.

THE FARMER'S SECOND BOOK, SABBATHDAY LAKE, MAINE *(1853)*

WHILE ACKNOWLEDGING the inherent beauty of many weeds, the Shakers regarded weeding as a spiritual exercise; they tolerated weeds in their gardens no more than they would tolerate impure thoughts in their minds. *The Gardener's Manual* exhorts: 'Weeding should be early performed, and continued with persevering faithfulness, as often as necessary, through the season.' One senses that the ceaseless weeding sometimes palled, no matter how good it may have been for the soul and the garden – one journal entry records 'With the gardeners it is weed weed hoe hoe because the weeds grow very fast.'

Hoeing, is usually the first act of cultivation in the garden which should be performed as soon as the plants are fairly up, and continued as necessary, for destroying weeds or nourishing the plants through the season, with punctuality and faithfulness.
THE GARDENER'S MANUAL

There were times during the growing season when the Shakers would have found my garden less than perfect. With seedlings and young plants I was scrupulous, and I made sure that I kept the perennial weeds at bay, but once the plants were well-established I weeded regularly, but not with 'persevering faithfulness'. As well as a hoe, I like to use a three-pronged claw to work in among the plants – there are fewer accidental beheadings with this tool! Ideally hoeing or hand-weeding is done in dry conditions as this discourages the weeds from re-establishing themselves. Any weeds left on the surface once they have been uprooted will shrivel and die.

Although the Shakers were rigorous in their removal of all weeds, the modern Shaker garden should be more tolerant as some weeds are important food and nectar plants for butterflies and beneficial insects. In my garden, outside the picket fence, well away from the raised beds, there is an area of rough grass where patches of nettles, thistles and clover are allowed to grow untouched by me unless they start to advance too close to the fence. This ensures the garden is enjoyed by both the butterflies and myself.

above
Weeds
The Shakers compared weeding the garden to ridding the soul of impure thoughts and believed the first would encourage the second.

Watering

SOME GARDENERS *spend much useless labor in sprinkling water over and around their plants. When the ground is very dry, at the time you wish to transplant, watering the ground where you intend to set the plants, a day or two beforehand, may be beneficial. But to plants in open ground, that have good roots, watering in the customary way, with a hand watering pot, is of but little use.*

THE GARDENER'S MANUAL

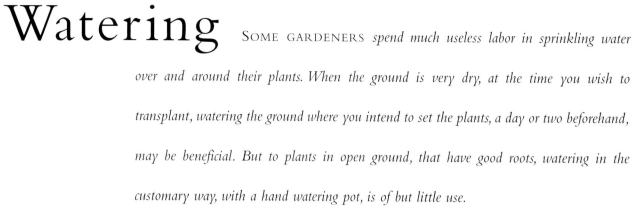

THE EARLY SHAKERS gardened at a time when watering was an onerous and time-consuming task with most water having to be carried by hand. Through their careful observation and recording of events in the garden they decided that hand-watering of an established crop was largely a wasted activity. They observed that once a plant was growing well with a good root system, this type of watering had little or no effect as the water seldom penetrates deep enough to be taken up by the plant.

This information is just as useful in today's Shaker garden. Light surface watering, by hand or hose, encourages the formation of surface roots, rather than the deeper roots which ensure that the plant can find moisture well below soil level, even in very dry weather. Constant watering creates soft, sappy plants that will quickly wither if water is withheld for any reason. Like children, plants need to be encouraged to be independent as they get older, by giving them a good start and the right environment in which they can flourish.

The Shaker advice on thoroughly watering the soil one or two days before transplanting in dry weather, is sound. This ensures that the soil will be evenly moist rather than wet in some places and dry in others as happens if the ground is watered immediately prior to transplanting.

Ideally watering should be carried out in the cool of the evening. This makes efficient use of the water as the plants can use the cool night-time hours to absorb it, before the sun evaporates the surface moisture. Water is a finite resource, and although it is far easier to water today's Shaker garden, it is essential that we make use of it in an economical and efficient way both for our future and that of generations to come.

above

Dolly tub

An old 'dolly' tub, precursor of the washing machine, has proved an excellent water butt for my Shaker garden. Topped up occasionally using the hose, it is an easily accessible water supply.

above

Wooden butt

A traditional wooden water butt tucked up against the trunk of a tree looks good, but it will need topping up with water regularly to ensure that it doesn't dry out and then cease to be watertight.

Barrel bung

*Wooden barrels
sometimes have a simple
bung rather than a tap.*

left

Evening watering

*Always water in the cool
of the evening or early
morning to avoid
scorching plants.*

Pests

TO BE SURE OF A CROP, *as all means of preventing the ravages of insects may at times fail, it is well to put in plenty of the seed of such plants as are attacked by them, which with the precautions heretofore given, to take means for having thrifty plants, is, in many instances, the only means of ensuring a crop.*

THE GARDENER'S MANUAL

GENERALLY THE SHAKER METHODS of insect control are a mixture of commonsense remedies familiar to today's organic gardeners, such as wood ash, salt and physical removal, and a rather alarming selection of potentially dangerous substances that we no longer use, such as quick lime and lye. Old fermented urine seems to have been a particular favourite, but however effective it may have proved I am not sure I would relish eating vegetables that had been treated with this particular type of insecticide!

The Shakers observed everything that happened in the garden and this allowed them to devise effective methods of control. For example they noted that the cutworm 'commits its depredations in the night; and immediately, on the appearance of day light, secretes itself under the dirt, near the plant which it last attacked.' This habit made it a relatively easy task to locate the grubs and destroy them before they damaged the beans, peppers, corn, onions, radishes and cabbages on which they preyed.

As a preventative, which is ever preferable to a cure, never put these vegetables on the same ground they occupied the previous year.

THE GARDENER'S MANUAL

right

Pest damage

It is essential to keep watch on plants and remove pests at the first sign of damage otherwise you can risk losing much of your crop. Slugs and snails come out in the evening or in damp weather, so these are the times that you need to be especially vigilant.

Like all good gardeners, the Shakers were aware that crop-rotation was an important way of controlling pests and keeping diseases at bay. Plants are more resistant to attack if they are inherently healthy, grown in good soil, well-spaced and weed-free and this was what the Shakers strove to achieve in their gardens.

However, regular crop rotation and plant vitality alone will not keep plants damage free. Vigilance is essential, and any problem is best dealt with early on before the pests have a chance to take hold. An evening patrol around the garden will help keep slugs and snails under control. How you dispose of them is up to you – personally I have a bucket of salt water at hand. The beginnings of a black fly attack on the runner beans in my Shaker garden was routed by using a high pressure water jet to wash them off, a treatment they clearly didn't like because they did not return. In general I try to use physical methods of control – barriers, companion planting or manually removing the pests, but more serious infestations may have to be treated using biological controls or organic insecticides.

Compost

THE BEST MANURE *for a garden is a compost, of one part mineral substances, as ashes, lime, sand or clay, (as the soil may require) salt, &c: five parts vegetable matter, as weeds, straw, leaves, roots and stalks of plants, and tan bark or sawdust to make the soil light, if necessary: and six parts of animal excrement. These should be collected in the course of the season, and mixed well together, to cause them to ferment. In the fall this compost should be spread evenly upon the garden, and ploughed in.*

THE GARDENER'S MANUAL

top left

Compost

Clockwise from top – commercial potting compost, well-rotted garden compost, loam.

top right

Mulch

clockwise from top – gravel, smooth pebbles and coarse grit all make good mulches.

THE MAKING OF COMPOST was central to the Shakers' way of gardening. They must have spent a great deal of time devising their recipe for the ideal compost as they worked to ensure the continuing soil fertility which was needed to keep their gardens productive. Their recipe allows for adjustments according to soil type and structure. The newly-cleared soils of New England were very acidic so the addition of lime would have been essential, but they recognised that soils vary enormously, so alternatives were suggested, both for the mineral and the vegetable content. The amount of compost added to the soil depended on its condition. Poor soil was enriched to the extent of 40 ox-cart loads per acre – an indication that their compost-making was on a massive scale.

The compost-making in my Shaker garden is on a more modest scale. As this is a newly established garden, there is no established compost heap, so it has been necessary to start from scratch. A simple wooden bin (see illustration) is the first of what will eventually be three bins ranged alongside one another. Once the first bin is

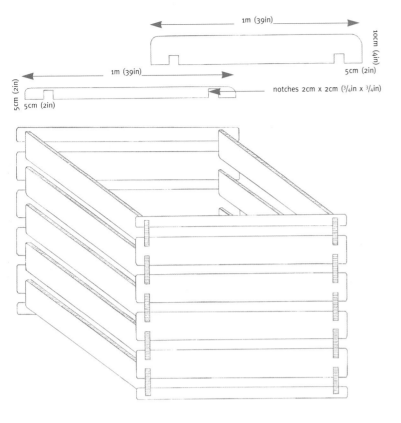

1m (39in)

10cm (4in)

5cm (2in)

1m (39in)

5cm (2in)

5cm (2in)

notches 2cm x 2cm (¾in x ¾in)

MAKING A COMPOST BIN

Materials & Equipment

For large planks:
18m (58½ft) of
10cm (4in) x 2cm (¾in)
wide timber
For narrow planks:
4m (13ft) of
5cm (2in) x 2cm (¾in)
wide timber

tenon saw

chisel

mallet

wood preservative

paintbrush

Method

1. For large planks, cut eighteen 1m (39in) lengths with 10cm (4in) width. For narrow planks, cut four 1m (39in) lengths with 5cm (2in) width.

2. Mark notches and cut out using saw and chisel

3. Paint timber with wood preservative

4. Place two narrow planks parallel on level ground 1m (39in) apart, notches upwards.

5. Slot un-notched side of 2 large planks into the notches to form a square. Use mallet if necessary.

6. Continue slotting in all the large planks. Finish with remaining narrow planks, notches downwards.

full, it will be covered and the contents left to rot down. The second bin and third bins will be added in turn, so that eventually I will have a bin of compost ready for use, a second full bin in the process of composting down, and a third bin ready to take fresh garden waste.

As far as possible I am following the Shaker recipe, although I have cut down on the amount of manure as this is not as readily available as it was for the Shakers, and I use a 50/50 mixture of lime and spent potting compost to make up the mineral content. The composting process works best when a substantial amount of fresh material is added in one go – otherwise the heap does not heat up effectively. All the ingredients should be thoroughly mixed together – I find this easier to do in a barrow before I put it in the bin.

The Shakers relied on the natural fertility of the soil and their compost to feed the plants. Today we also use liquid feeds, and in my Shaker garden I use a dilute seaweed feed to keep plants growing strongly. There are a number of these liquids available to the organic gardener, or you could make your own from comfrey or nettles by immersing the freshly cut leaves in a tub of water and leaving them to rot down for six weeks. At the end of this time you can use the (very smelly) brown liquid as a highly effective liquid feed.

Mulches were not favoured by the Shakers who preferred the purity of bare soil. Mulches were only used to provide winter protection for plants and were removed to the compost heap in the spring, but I shall in future use compost as a mulch as I consider it to be an effective way of conserving moisture and suppressing weeds.

right

Compost bin

Be sure to position the compost bin in an easily accessible place, close to the garden, or you will make more work for yourself.

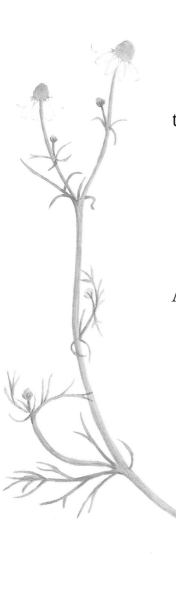

" Behold *the Flowers* that deck the Field,

the Gentle breeze *perfuming,*

And *Tender* Herbs their *Fragrance Yield*

Are Health and Life Defusing. "

Herb catalogue - *Harvard Community, Massachusetts, 1843.*

herbs

Matricaria recutita
syn. Matricaria chamomilla

There were herbs of many kinds. *Lobelia, pennyroyal, spearmint, peppermint, catnip, wintergreen, thoroughwort, sarsaparilla and dandelion grew wild in the surrounding fields. When it was time to harvest them, an elderly Brother would take a great wagonload of children, armed with tow sheets to the pastures. Here they would pick the appointed herbs, each one had its own day, that there might be no danger of mixing, and, when their sheets were full, drive solemnly home again.*

SISTER MARCIA BULLARD, GOOD HOUSEKEEPING *(1906)*

T O THE SHAKERS the value of herbs lay primarily in their medicinal qualities – their culinary use was very limited indeed. At a time when the accepted medical treatment was frequently more deadly than the illness itself, the Shakers turned to the plant remedies of the Native Americans, initially to ensure their own health, and eventually to establish a profitable and well-respected business that was the foundation of much of their prosperity. With their scrupulous attention to detail, meticulous working methods and honesty they quickly developed an unrivalled reputation for pure, high quality herbs that they sold in huge quantities.

In the early Shaker settlements the majority of the herbs were gathered from the wild, supplemented by the small-scale cultivation of a few familiar varieties brought from the old country. These herbs were used to keep the communities healthy, combined with the faith-healing and laying-on-of-hands used by Mother Ann and, in later years, a variety of therapies that were popular in 'the World' at the time such as emetics, purges and fasting.

Small quantities may have been sold to outsiders, but it wasn't until 1820 that the herb business proper was started. New Lebanon was the first settlement to establish the practice of large-scale cultivation of herbs. By the 1850's this community was producing up to 100,000 pounds of dried herbs annually and other herbal products as indicated by their catalogue of 1851: *A catalogue of Medicinal Plants, Barks, Roots, Seeds, Flowers and Select Powders with their Therapeutic Qualities and Botanical names; also Pure Vegetable Extracts, prepared in vacuo; Ointments, Inspissated Juices, Essential Oils,*

Double Distilled and Fragrant Waters, etc., Raised, Prepared and Put up in the most Careful Manner by the United Society of Shakers at New Lebanon, N.Y.

The catalogue contains an endorsement by Constantine Rafinesque – the author of *Medical Flora, or a Manual of the Medical Botany of the United States in North America* – 'The best medical gardens in the United States are those established by the communities of the Shakers.'

Other Shaker communities followed New Lebanon, and large-scale production was established at Canterbury, Watervliet, Harvard and Union Village. Eventually there were around 200 acres of physic gardens in the various communities. At the Hancock settlement there was a 10-acre herb garden, four acres of which were used solely for sage, one of their most popular remedies and one of the few herbs also widely used in the kitchen.

opposite

Herbs by a dwelling

Herbs growing round the door of a house at the Canterbury Shaker Village.

above

Victorian garden

The growing of plants close to Shaker houses was fairly unusual until Victorian times.

Medicinal Herbs

JULY 14TH, 15TH. *Working in physic garden, here a little, and there a little, but don't fret. August gathering herbs here and there, go on west hills after lobelia. 26th and 27th work in medical garden, 30th and 31st gathering bugle here and there. Sept 1830 spend this month gathering herbs and roots here and there, up hill and down. 22nd, 23rd and 24th, down to Sheffield after blue cohosh, 28th on the mountain after maidenhair.*

BENJAMIN GATES, NEW LEBANON 1830

KEY

1. Mullein
2. St. John's wort
3. Feverfew
4. Peppermint
5. German chamomile
6. Marigold
7. Roman chamomile
8. Golden hop
9. Hollyhock
10. Cone flower
11. Sage
12. Rosa gallica
13. Rosa damascena
14. Comfrey
15. Common thyme

right

Plan of herb garden

This garden contains a selection of the safer plants which the Shakers grew for medicinal purposes. Some are still used in home remedies.

MEDICINAL HERB GARDEN

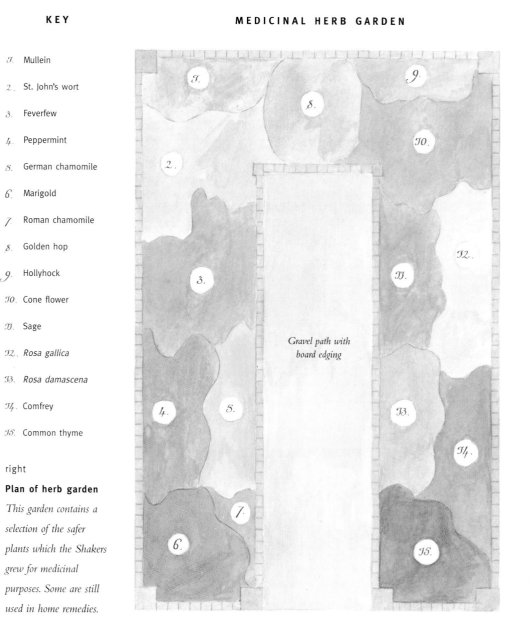

Gravel path with board edging

THERE IS A note of exasperation in Benjamin Gates' description of his work – so many 'here and there's' indicates that perhaps he would have preferred a little less variety in his work – but it was the obedience and care with which the Shakers undertook their work that ensured that their herbs were pure and of the highest quality.

They would be collected at different times of the year depending on the part of the herb that was to be used medicinally. Roots were lifted in the autumn and cleaned and dried indoors. Fragile parts of the herbs were gathered on 15ft square tow sheets. The flowers were considered the most valuable part of the plants and were gathered when they first opened and dried quickly to keep their colour. Leaves were picked when the flowers bloomed.

Harvesting was always done early in the morning, after the dew had dried, but before the heat of the sun started to

RECIPE

HEALING HAND BALM

*A lanolin-rich hand balm which can be
applied before gardening to protect the hands or
afterwards to soothe and nourish hands which
may be sore or cracked.*

Ingredients

25g (1oz) lanolin

15g (1/2oz) white beeswax

75g (3oz) almond oil

50ml (2 fl oz) pure water

10 drops chamomile oil

5 drops geranium oil

5 drops lemon oil

Method

Gently melt the lanolin and beeswax in a double
boiler. While whisking the mixture, slowly add the
almond oil – it will start to thicken and become
opaque. Continue whisking and add the water a few
drops at a time. The mixture will emulsify and become
a thick cream. Stir in the essential oils and pour the
balm into a clean, lidded container.

top

Hand balm

*Keep a lidded
earthenware or pottery
dish of hand balm next to
the sink or tap where you
wash your hands after
gardening so that you can
apply some immediately.
The essential oils included
make it mildly antiseptic.*

above

Pure ingredients

*Pure, simple ingredients
which would have been
familiar to the Shakers
have been blended with
essential oils to make a
healing balm – purified
white beeswax, lanolin
and almond oil are
effective and inexpensive.*

evaporate the oils in the plants. Biennial
plants such as foxgloves were harvested in
their second year of growth. Bark was
gathered at the time of rising sap in the
fall or spring; to avoid damaging the tree,
this was done by removing selected
branches so as not to harm the remainder
of the tree. Seeds were ripened in the sun
and gathered as soon as they were ripe to
avoid predation by birds and other animals.

The herbs were processed in specially
-built buildings. At New Lebanon the
Herb House had drying rooms on the
second floor and in the attic, while in
another part of the building a horse-
powered press compacted leaves and roots
into solid cakes. Herbs were distilled in
the Extract House and elsewhere the
Finishing Room was used for packaging
and labelling. An article in *Harper's* magazine
in 1857 notes that 'in every department
perfect order and neatness prevail. System
is everywhere observed, and all operations
are carried on with exact economy.'

HYPERICUM — ST. JOHN'S WORT   CHRYSANTHEMUM PARTHENIUM — FEVERFEW   CALENDULA OFFICINALIS — MARIGOLD

Medicinal Herb Glossary

WHAT IS THE RELEVANCE *of the Shaker physic gardens to today's gardeners? It would not be in keeping with the Shaker philosophy to plant an historically accurate medicinal garden that was for viewing only. However, all but the safest plants should be used with extreme caution and only with professional guidance. In planning my medicinal herb garden I have selected 15 plants, most of which can be safely used as natural remedies, and a few of which I would not recommend for home use, but which are historically accurate and help give the garden structure and form.*

HOLLYHOCK *Alcea rosea*

The Shakers recommended the use of the hollyhock for female complaints and coughs. This tall-growing biennial (or the short-lived perennial) is best grown from seed and then planted out in full sun, preferably against a wall or fence. It does not have a modern medicinal use, but is such a lovely plant that I have included it anyway.

POT MARIGOLD *Calendula officinalis*

Ointments and tinctures were made from marigolds by the Shakers for the treatment of cuts, sores and insect bites. Marigolds are annual plants that grow very easily from seed. They can be sown direct into the soil and thinned out as necessary or started off in pots for planting out later. *Calendula* cream can be used to treat cuts and sores.

ROMAN CHAMOMILE *Chamaemelum nobile* (syn. *Anthemis nobilis*)

This variety of chamomile is listed by the Shakers as being used to treat nausea and as a sedative. It is effective for this, but has a bitter taste compared with the equally effective German chamomile.

Roman chamomile is an evergreen perennial that forms a mat and bears white daisy flowers from spring until late summer. Nowadays Roman chamomile is used primarily as an ingredient in shampoos and hair rinses for fair hair and as an ingredient in pot pourris.

CONE FLOWER *Echinacea purpurea*

The Native Americans considered *echinacea* to be a universal panacea, so it is likely that the Shakers would have cultivated this plant in their physic gardens. It is a perennial plant with lance-shaped leaves and large purple-pink flowers and prefers to be grown in fertile, well-drained soil in full sun. Modern research has shown that echinacea is a powerful immune system stimulant that seems to have no side-effects. Treatment uses powdered root taken from plants of at least three to four years growth and should be undertaken only with professional guidance and using powders processed under laboratory conditions.

GOLDEN HOP *Humulus lupulus* 'Aureus'

A simple extract of hops was made by the Shakers who recommended it as a sedative. The golden hop is a more attractive variant of the ordinary hop. It is a strong-growing perennial that can be trained over an arch or fence and will grow in sun or shade in well-drained soil. A hop-filled sachet slipped under the pillow is said to induce sleep.

ST JOHN'S WORT *Hypericum perforatum*

The Shakers made a rich red lotion from St John's Wort. It was used to soothe rough skin or sores by soaking the freshly-picked flowers in alcohol or oil. *Hypericum perforatum* is a clump-forming perennial which grows easily in well-drained soil in a sunny position. In recent years St John's Wort has been recognised as an effective antidepressant and is now prescribed by doctors. Do not attempt self-medication for this condition.

GERMAN CHAMOMILE *Matricaria recutita*

It is not certain that the Shakers grew this variety of annual chamomile but no modern medicinal herb garden should be without it as it is far superior to the Roman chamomile for internal consumption. See page 80 for cultivation notes.

ECHINACEA – CONE FLOWER

SYMPHYTUM OFFICINALE – BORAGE

OENOTHERA MISSOURIENSIS – EVENING PRIMROSE

PEPPERMINT *Mentha piperita vulgaris*

The soothing effect of peppermint on the digestive system has been known for hundreds of years. The Shakers, like many others, used the herb as an effective treatment for stomach-ache, easing nausea and reducing colic. Peppermint was also distilled to make a flavouring to disguise unpleasant tasting medicines. It is a vigorous, spreading perennial, which will do well in sun or shade in well-drained soil. As it is invasive it is best planted in a container such as an old bucket that is then sunk into the soil. Avoid peppermint when taking homeopathic remedies as it interferes with their action.

ROSE *Rosa gallica officinalis & Rosa damascena*

Medicinally, rosa gallica was the Shaker's favourite rose for its mildly astringent and tonic effects. *Rosa damascena* was one of the three other roses they grew, the others being *Rosa alba* and *Rosa centifolia*. Rose water was one of their most important products and was sold to 'the World' as a flavouring and for use in perfumes.

Rosa gallica is a neat, bushy rose with semi-double, pinky-red flowers. Recommended varieties of *Rosa damascena* are 'Gloire de Guilan', which was grown in Persia for the production of attar of roses, and 'Ispahan' with its richly fragrant double pink flowers. Roses should be planted in a sunny position in soil enriched with bonemeal and farmyard manure. The petals from these roses can be dried for pot pourri.

SAGE *Salvia officinalis*

Sow in drills 2 feet apart, and thin to 8 or 10 inches in the row. It is a perennial; but as young plants produce the best leaves, it should be resown once in 2 years.

THE GARDENER'S MANUAL

The Shakers prescribed sage for colds and coughs and also for night-sweats. For full notes on cultivation see page 81. Modern research indicates that sage has many medicinal properties including those listed by the Shakers. It is now also believed to have a significant effect in delaying the onset of Alzheimer's disease if taken regularly.

COMFREY *Symphytum officinale*

Comfrey was listed by the Shakers as a treatment for dropsy, dysentery and sores in the *Druggists' Handbook of Pure Botanic Preparations* (1873). It is a vigorous perennial with large lance-shaped leaves and cream or blue flowers. The hairy leaves can irritate the skin. It does best in moist soil in sun or partial shade; as it can prove invasive its roots should be restricted. Today comfrey is used primarily as a plant food (see page 65) or as a green manure for the compost heap.

CREEPING THYME *Thymus serpyllum*

Thyme was one of the few herbs that the Shakers used in cooking, but they also used it for the treatment of headaches and hysteria. Thyme is a Mediterranean herb and most varieties need to be grown in pots or treated as an annual in colder regions. Creeping thyme, however, tolerates shade

and moisture better than the other varieties and is recorded as growing in the orchard at Harvard. It has successfully naturalised itself in the areas around Shaker settlements in Massachusetts and adjoining states. Thyme is little used medicinally nowadays, although a thyme infusion is a pleasant aid to digestion.

FEVERFEW *Tanacetum parthenium*

According to the *Hancock Shaker Village Herb Guide*, the Shakers used feverfew to treat colds and worms. It is an attractive biennial with deeply-lobed leaves on a bushy plant and daisy-like white flowers. It grows readily and will self-seed freely. Sandwiches made with feverfew leaves as a filling are reputed to be effective in treating some migraine headaches.

MULLEIN *Verbascum densiflorum* (syn. *V.thapsiforme*)

Mullein was used by the Shakers to treat chest and ear infections. It is an attractive, tall-growing biennial plant with a rosette of felty grey leaves from which emerge tall spires of pale yellow flowers. It grows well in a sunny position, preferably near the back of a border and self-seeds readily. It was once known as the candlewick plant because the tall flower spikes were dipped into tallow to make primitive torches. Medicinally the flowers are considered superior, but the leaves and roots can also be used. A tea that is said to have sedative properties may be brewed from the fresh flowers and leaves.

Culinary Herbs

To preserve Sweet, Pot and Medicinal herbs and flowers, they should be gathered when in bloom, thoroughly dried and put up in tight boxes or jars, till wanted for use.

THE GARDENER'S MANUAL

THE FIRST APPEARANCE of culinary herbs, or sweet herbs as they were known in the Shaker catalogues, was in 1847, six years later than the medicinal herbs. To differentiate the culinary herbs from the medicinal ones, they were sold in small metal canisters rather than compressed blocks. This was at a time when the Shakers made dramatic

above

Containers of herbs

Culinary herbs can be grown in the smallest garden.

right

Herb honey

Honey scented with thyme flowers.

opposite top

Sweet marjoram

Sweet marjoram was one of a limited selection of Shaker culinary herbs.

opposite

Thyme flowers

The flowers of thyme are milder than the leaves.

RECIPE

HERB HONEY

A commercial blended honey can be given a deliciously distinctive flavour if culinary herbs, or even better, herb flowers are added to it.

Ingredients

a jar of clear honey

1 tablespoon of tender thyme tips complete with flowers

Method

Pick thyme tips early in the day. Wash gently and leave to dry. Stir into the honey. Seal the jar and stand the honey in a warm place for 1 week, stirring occasionally to allow the flavour to permeate through the honey. Serve in the usual way.

parsley seed was a remedy for head lice. Although *The Gardener's Manual* refers to it, there seems to be little reference to it having been used in food except as a pot herb (a selection of greens cooked together) until Mary Whitcher's *Shaker House-Keeper* was published in 1882. Similarly basil, much loved by 20th century cooks, was a remedy for excessive vomiting, and an infusion of rosemary was used to treat colds, colic and nervous complaints. As the popularity of medicinal herbs waned the Shaker sisters started to use them in other ways. Candies were made from sweet flag, horehound and lovage and refreshing herbal drinks were taken out to the fields at haying time. In her book *Shaker Your Plate*, Sister Frances Carr, for 40 years the Kitchen Deaconess at Sabbathday Lake, lists 21 culinary herbs, but she recalls that there was very little 'herb cooking' in the village when she was a child.

changes to their diet, eschewing the earlier meat-rich, high fat foods, which were now perceived as harmful. They adopted and adapted a diet based on the nutritional theories of Sylvester Graham, the inventor of the Graham cracker and an early advocate of wholegrain bread and vegetarian food. It is likely that they started to add herbs to these new, rather bland foods to make them more interesting and also to help protect the communities from dyspepsia (indigestion), which was a fairly universal problem at the time.

The early Shakers used a limited repertoire of sweet herbs – thyme, summer savory, sweet marjoram and less frequently, horseradish. Many of the herbs that we commonly use in our food today were valued primarily for their medicinal properties. Parsley, for instance, was used for many purposes – parsley root was used to treat dropsy, water retention and venereal disease, the leaves for insect stings and bites and

ROSMARINUS OFFICINALIS – ROSEMARY

OCIMUM BASILICUM – BASIL

MENTHA SPICATA – SPEARMINT

Culinary Herb Glossary

TODAY WE USE *a far wider repertoire of culinary herbs than the Shakers; we have become familiar with herbs that have their origins the world over and incorporate them in our food to an extent that would have astonished them. In choosing culinary herbs for the Shaker garden I decided to limit myself mainly to herbs that would have been familiar to the Shakers even if they would not have used them in the way we do.*

SPEARMINT *Mentha spicata*

Although primarily used for medicinal purposes – to control colic, vomiting and dropsy – the Shakers did make mint sauce to accompany lamb. It is likely that the recipe was brought from England by the earliest Shakers as the sauce is made the traditional English way with vinegar, sugar and hot water. Spearmint is one of the easiest herbs to grow, provided the roots are planted in moist, rich soil in partial shade. Because it is an invasive plant it should be grown in a container or where its root run can be restricted. Mint is delicious added to salads or steamed with new potatoes.

BASIL *Ocimum basilicum*

Basil was used solely as a medicinal herb by the Shakers who used it to prevent vomiting. Basil is an annual that needs warm conditions for the seed to germinate and should be started off indoors or sown outdoors in warm weather once all risk of frost has gone. Basil dislikes root disturbance so sow thinly whether in pots or outdoors. I sowed basil seeds outdoors and in pots and found that, on the whole, the pot-grown plants did far better because they did not have to compete for space in the same way as they did in the Shaker garden. Basil is the perfect partner for tomatoes.

SWEET MARJORAM *Origanum vulgare*

The Shakers used sweet marjoram in stuffings and as a flavouring for soups, stews and meat dishes. They grew it as an annual although *The Gardener's Manual* refers to it as a biennial – in milder regions it can be grown as a short-lived perennial.

Sweet marjoram is a hardy biennial, a native of Portugal. Sow about 1st of May broadcast on a bed prepared – have the ground made very fine, and sow the seed on the same without any drilling. The seed will not want any covering, lay a board on the bed and walk on it, which will be all that is necessary to ensure it to vegetate. When the plant becomes large enough to transplant, set them at a distance of six inches. Water the plants if the weather is dry. When in blossom the herb is cut over, and dried for winter use, so that a sowing requires to be made every year. The herb is much used in soups, broths, stuffings &c.

THE GARDENER'S MANUAL

When grown as a perennial, sweet marjoram does best when positioned in full sun in free-draining soil. Old growth should be cut back in autumn. I have planted an old fashioned wash-tub with a variety of sun-loving herbs including sweet marjoram and it is positioned in a sheltered spot close to my kitchen door. Today sweet marjoram is used to enliven red meat dishes, is an essential flavouring in sausagemeat and helps give pizzas their authentic flavour.

PARSLEY *Petroselinum*

A salutary pot herb. Cultivate the same as early lettuce.

THE GARDENER'S MANUAL

Once the Shakers had adopted parsley as a culinary herb they used it on salads and to make a sauce that was served with fish or poultry. In the Shaker garden, I grew both the curly-leaved parsley and the flat-leaved variety, which I consider to have a better flavour. Although biennial plants, they are normally grown from seed each year as annuals.

Parsley grows best in light shade in soil enriched with manure or compost. I planted curly

ORIGANUM MARJORANA – SWEET MARJORAM

PETROSELINUM – FLAT LEAVED PARSLEY

SALVIA OFFICINALIS 'ICTERINA' – SAGE

parsley alongside a row of turnips so that the herb could grow in their shade. As well as enhancing salads, cooked vegetables and casseroles, parsley is extremely rich in chlorophyll, which makes it an excellent breath freshener, and recent research seems to indicate that it can reduce cholesterol levels if eaten regularly.

ROSEMARY *Rosmarinus officinalis*

The Shakers did not use rosemary as a culinary herb, reserving it instead for the treatment of coughs and colds. It is an attractive evergreen herb with blue flowers that appear early in the year, and sometimes again in the autumn. It is a herb that is particularly susceptible to a combination of cold and wet and in colder zones is best grown as a container plant with winter protection. Elsewhere, rosemary should be positioned in full sun and planted in a free-draining soil. It should be trimmed regularly to maintain its shape as it will not regrow from old wood. In cooking it is used to flavour lamb, roast vegetables and savoury breads.

SAGE *Salvia officinalis*

The Shakers used more sage than any other herb in their cooking. It was much used to flavour and preserve sausage meat and in the stuffings for turkey and chicken.

This useful herb requires a good rich soil, and may be sown in drills, about two feet apart, when of sufficient size for culinary purposes, it may be thinned out as it is wanted. The plants intended to be kept over the winter may finally be left at the distance of two feet each way. They may stand through the winter covered with straw or litter or they may be taken up and put in the cellar. After the first year they will grow and bear seed a number of years in succession, but new seed should be sown once in three or four years as young roots produce the most thrifty shoots.

THE GARDENER'S MANUAL

In climates milder than that of New England, sage plants will stand through the winter without protection. Plant in full sun in free-draining soil. The plants should be pinched out regularly throughout the growing season to prevent them becoming 'leggy'. Bearing in mind the Shaker fondness for this herb, I planted six sage plants in my Shaker garden resulting in far more sage than I can use – one or two plants will be ample for the average garden. Sage is still popular as a flavouring for pork and an ingredient in stuffings. Fried briefly in butter, sage leaves are delicious sprinkled on pasta dishes and the flowers add colour and flavour to salads, but use only the petals, not the calyx.

SUMMER SAVOURY *Satureja hortensis*

This herb is a traditional flavouring for all types of beans, fresh or dried, and was believed by the Shakers to make any bean dish more digestible.

This plant will grow in almost any soil. It may be sown in drills about twelve or fourteen inches apart so as to pass a hoe freely between the rows. Let it be kept clean from weeds – and if it comes up too thick, let it be gradually thinned out as it is wanted for use, and it will not require any further trouble. To dry it for winter use, it should be cut when in blossom and spread on the floor of an upper room or garret, where it can have air, and not be exposed to the sun. When it is sufficiently dry, tie it up in bunches, and wrap it in paper, or put it away in clean bags for future use.

THE GARDENER'S MANUAL

Summer Savoury does best when grown in full sun. It is a herb that dries particularly well, losing none of its pungency in the process. Young broad beans lightly flavoured with summer savory are quite delicious.

LEMON THYME *Thymus citriodorus*

Thymus serpyllum, the variety of thyme usually grown by the Shakers, is listed in the previous section on medicinal herbs, but I have included lemon thyme here because it is superior as a culinary herb. It is another herb that does not like the cold or wet – if in any doubt, bring it undercover in the winter and water sparingly. Thyme does best in gritty soil, baked by the sun. The Shakers used thyme to flavour meat dishes. Today it is most frequently used as an ingredient in bouquets garnis.

Tisane herbs

No kind of ardent spirits *may be used among Believers, as a beverage, nor on any occasion except by order of the Physicians.*

THE MILLENNIAL LAWS

RECIPE

EARL GREY &
LEMON VERBENA TEA

A delicious and fragrant afternoon tea which can be drunk like a tisane or chilled and sweetened for use as an iced tea.

Ingredients

1 heaped teaspoon Earl Grey tea

6 lemon verbena leaves

0.5 litre (1 pint) boiling water

Method

Place the Earl Grey tea and the lemon verbena leaves in a previously warmed teapot and pour on the boiling water. Infuse for 5 minutes before serving.

REFRESHING and health-giving teas were popular drinks in Shaker Communities at a time when 'ardent spirits' were forbidden. The tradition of drinking infusions of herbs such as chamomile and mint had originally been brought from the old world. This tradition was further enriched by the addition of new plants like bergamot, *Monarda didyma*, which were introduced to the Shakers by the Native Americans. A popular tea among the Shakers known as Steeplebush or Hardhack was made from meadowsweet, *Spiraea tomentosa*, and another, Liberty or New Jersey Tea came from American ceanothus.

Tisanes have enjoyed a renaissance in recent years as we have sought to avoid the harmful effects of caffeine, sugary drinks and 'ardent spirits', and most homes will have a selection of commercially produced herb teas in their kitchen cupboard. Many of these herbs are easy to grow and you can establish your own tisane garden however limited your space may be.

Making a tisane from freshly picked herbs is simplicity itself. Pick a few leaves, wash them carefully under cold running water and then put them into a small teapot or mug. Pour over recently boiled water (not boiling) and leave to infuse for 5–10 minutes. If you are making the tisane in a mug or cup you should cover it with a saucer while it infuses or the essential oils from the herbs will evaporate away and the flavour will be less intense. A tisane can be sweetened with honey or sugar, but most tisanes are delicious without added sweetness.

Each herb can be used on its own to make a tisane or blended with other herbs or even conventional teas. Those who find the flavour of chamomile unpalatable may like to experiment with blending it with mint in different proportions until the right balance is found.

In warm weather herb teas can be drunk cold, either on their own or with the addition of ice cubes and a sprig of fresh herbs, as a delicious, refreshing and healthy drink.

left

Lemon verbena

The queen of all tisane herbs, the leaves of the lemon verbena, Aloysia triphylla, *make a fragrant and refreshing drink, delicious drunk hot or cold.*

below

Spearmint

Mentha spicata *is more delicately flavoured than peppermint. Mint tea is soothing to the digestive system, and a gentle pick-me-up when tired.*

above

Sage

The Shakers grew more sage than any other herb. The purple sage, Salvia officinalis 'Purpurascens' *is both decorative and recommended as a tea, taken with honey, to soothe sore throats.*

right

Bergamot

The flowering bracts of Monarda didyma *look more like a warning than an invitation, but infused with the leaves they make Oswego tea.*

MENTHA SPICATA — SPEARMINT

FOENICULUM VULGARE — FENNEL

Tisane Herb Glossary

LEMON VERBENA *Aloysia triphylla*
(syn. *Aloysia citriodora* syn. *Lippia citriodora*)
The most refreshing of all tisanes is made from the leaves of the lemon verbena. It is reputed to soothe the mucous membranes but its delicious taste is such that once tasted you will not need to find an ailment before you drink it again. Lemon verbena leaves dry very successfully and when used to make a tisane will immediately regain the appearance of fresh leaves.

Lemon verbena is hardy in only the mildest of climates where it should be planted in poor soil and watered sparingly. Otherwise it is really a greenhouse or conservatory plant, which can be stood outdoors in the mild summer months. Pruning should be done in the spring when the new growth starts to appear.

FENNEL *Foeniculum vulgare*
Fennel tea is wonderfully soothing to the digestive system, will allay hiccups, sweeten the breath and act as an appetite suppressant.

Fennel is a lovely plant that should have a place in every garden. The bronze fennel is particularly attractive and can be used in exactly the same way as the common green fennel. It grows well in any sunny, fertile position. The leaves, flower heads and seeds can all be used to make tisanes of varying strengths, although the seeds have the most concentrated flavour. In the autumn as the growth dies back, cut back the stems to 10cm (4in). In cold regions it is advisable to dig up the roots and store them in a frost-free place over winter or cover the plants with a thick protective mulch.

CHAMOMILE *Matricaria recutita* (syn. *Matricaria chamomilla*)
Chamomile tea is best known as a soothing bedtime drink. It is an acquired taste, but it is worth persevering, as its calming and sedative properties are entirely free of side-effects.

Chamomile comes in several shapes and forms and has many confusing names. The German chamomile, *Matricaria recutita (syn. Matricaria chamomilla)*, is the one used for tisanes and herbal medicines, and is an annual grown from seed.

The seeds are very fine, and are best mixed with sand for sowing, which can be done in spring or autumn, preferably in damp conditions. Once you have established German chamomile in the garden it will self-seed readily, although not necessarily where you want it to, but as this is a plant that is good for the health of the garden as well as your own, it is worth tolerating even if this compromises Shaker orderliness. Chamomile will flower eight weeks after planting between May and October. The flowers can be harvested when they are fully open in warm, dry weather. Dry in a single layer on a rack in a warm, airy room. Avoid touching as they crumble easily. When fully dry store in the dark in an airtight container. Use one teaspoon of dried chamomile flowers per serving.

BERGAMOT *Monarda didyma*
Oswego tea, also known as Bee Balm, was a favourite drink of the Native Americans who introduced this herb to the Shakers. It has to be said that it smells better than it actually tastes, although perhaps, like chamomile, it is a taste that can be acquired. The flavour of the petals is slightly gentler than that of the leaves. It is reputed to have a soothing and relaxing effect. Both leaves and flowers dry successfully.

Bergamot likes rich, moist soil and will not thrive in full sun. Ideally it should be split annually in late summer. Discard the centre of the plant and use the fresh young shoots from the edges.

LEMON BALM *Melissa officinalis*
If lemon verbena proves difficult to grow, you can grow lemon balm instead, although the tea will be markedly less lemony. The Shakers used it to dispel mild fevers.

Like mint, lemon balm can be difficult to control once it gets a foothold. To keep it in order it is advisable to dig it up in early autumn, split it, and replant every two or three years. It also self-seeds very readily. The young plants are quite easy to remove but can be more difficult if given time to get established. Lemon balm will grow in most soils and most conditions, but does best in partial shade — too much sun and the leaves yellow, too little and it is less aromatic. In the autumn it should be cut right back and given a mulch of compost. In colder zones lemon balm must be grown from seed annually. Trim regularly to prevent flowering.

MONARDA DIDYMA – BERGAMOT

SPEARMINT *Mentha spicata*

Mint tea is universally popular and its use long pre-dates the Shakers. Its refreshing qualities are reason enough to drink it, but it is also beneficial to the digestive system and effectively quells nausea.

Mint is one of the easiest of all herbs to grow, the problem with mint is confining it, because once established it tends to develop imperialist tendencies. In a Shaker garden, or any other garden for that matter, it is best grown in a container or in a bed that has had slate pushed down around its perimeter to prevent it escaping. Mint should be planted in rich soil in partial shade as it prefers a cool root run. Water regularly in dry weather. When picking mint, leave 10cm (4in) of the stem intact to grow new shoots. In the autumn cut the plant right back and top-dress with good quality compost. You can also pot up a few roots to bring indoors to provide mint during the winter months.

PURPLE SAGE *Salvia officinalis purpurascens*

Sage tea was popular in medieval times as its consumption was believed to promote mental agility in old age (hence its name). Recent research would appear to confirm that this is the case and that regular drinking of sage tea may be effective in preventing senile dementia and Alzheimer's disease. The Native Americans used sage infusions for coughs, colds and nervous complaints and it was a favoured remedy of the Shakers. They grew the common grey sage, *salvia officinalis*, but purple sage is now believed to be more effective. When used to relieve coughs, colds and sore throats add honey to the tisane. Dry the leaves in a cool, airy place for winter use.

Sage likes to be grown in full sun in well-drained soil. Coarse grit should be added to heavy soils. In milder climates it is quite hardy, but in colder regions follow the Shaker example and earth-up the plants or lift and store them in a root-cellar over winter. The following year the roots can be divided up and planted out. Sage can also be propagated from heel cuttings or by layering. After 4 or 5 years, sage plants weaken and are best replaced.

"Forty years ago *it was* contrary *to the* 'Orders' which *governed our lives* to *cultivate useless flowers*, but *fortunately* for those of us who loved them, there are *many* plants *which are* beautiful *as well as* useful."

Sister Marcia Bullard,

GOOD HOUSEKEEPING

(July 1906)

flowers

Tropaeolum majus

'The rose bushes were planted *along the sides of the road which ran through our village and were greatly admired by the passer-by, but it was strongly impressed upon us that a rose was useful not ornamental. It was not intended to please us by its color or its odor, its mission was to be made into rose-water, and if we thought of it in any other way we were making an idol of it and thereby imperiling our souls.'*

SISTER MARCIA BULLARD

As this quote amply demonstrates, the Shakers mistrusted anything that was purely decorative. Although *The Millennial Laws 1845* did not actually forbid the growing of flowers, most of the communities appear to have restricted them to those blooms for which a use could be found. It is clear that even the habitually obedient Shakers sometimes found the restrictions on what they could do burdensome, and there appears to be a rare glimpse of rebellion when Sister Bullard recalls that 'fortunately for those of us who loved them, there are many plants which are beautiful as well as useful.' From our modern perspective it is sad to think of those early Shaker gardeners fearing that a moment of pleasure derived from the sight or scent of a beautiful flower might imperil their souls, but in the context of the times in which they lived such a prohibition was not unusual.

After the Civil War, the Shakers became far more relaxed about what could and could not be grown, and archive photos clearly show the once plain surroundings of the dwelling houses increasingly adorned by encroaching flower gardens and even flower-covered trellises and porches. This change coincided with the slow but inevitable decline in the number of men in the Shaker movement. It may well have been the increasingly female membership that permitted flowers to be picked and brought indoors and came to regard flower gardening as a suitable recreation for the sisters and young girls. It is also a reflection of the increasing 'Victorianisation' of Shaker life.

Where the Shakers had previously concentrated on producing seed for medicinal herbs and vegetables, at the Canterbury community they began to grow ornamental flowers for seed. These seeds, in colourful packets, found a ready market in 'the World' and there are records of many varieties including sweet peas, hollyhocks, sweet alyssum, zinnias and petunias.

opposite
Useful roses

Roses were always harvested without their stems to ensure that no one was tempted to pin a blossom to their dress or stand the flower in a vase.

left
Flower harvest

The children of the settlements were an important part of the workforce and the girls were regularly employed picking flowers. The flowers may have looked lovely in the fields but it was still back-breaking work.

Flowers for Drying

'WE ALWAYS HAD *extensive poppy beds and early in the morning, before the sun had risen, the white-capped sisters could be seen stooping among the scarlet blossoms to slit these pods from which the petals had just fallen.'*

SISTER MARCIA BULLARD

above from left to right

Peony

Peony 'Sarah Bernhardt' dries a deep pink.

Tansy

Tansy flowers retain their strong yellow when dried.

Cardoon

A highly decorative relative of the artichoke.

THIS DESCRIPTION OF THE SHAKER sisters working among the poppy flowers conjures up an impressionistically beautiful image. It is tempting to romanticise their lives, but the reality is that they were engaged in hard, back-breaking work preparing the seed-heads for the harvesting of opium, which was an important medicinal crop. The decorative appearance of the poppy heads would have had no relevance to the task in which they were engaged.

There were many other flowers grown and dried for use in medicines, tinctures and floral waters. Daffodils, larkspur, marigold, statice, bergamot, sweet marjoram and tansy are among those listed in the 1850 *Annual Wholesale Catalogue* from Union Village, Ohio. The cultivation was carried out by the men, while the collecting and drying was done by the women and children. The harvested flowers were taken to the herb house for cleaning and were processed or dried on racks, or in a kiln, before being compressed and packaged ready for sale.

Today we dry flowers for their long-lasting beauty – and truth-be-told – it is difficult to think of anything less functional than a bunch of dried flowers; but with their pragmatic and commercial approach to 'the World', the Shakers would probably have appreciated that there was money-making potential and proceeded to dry flowers better than anyone else!

The flowers I have selected for use in a Shaker garden are all plants with which the Shakers would have been familiar even though they would have put them to different use. Rather than plant an area specifically for this purpose, these flowers have been incorporated into perennial planting.

Once you have successfully mastered the techniques used to dry flowers you will find that the resultant blooms are far superior to the majority that can be bought in stores. Their natural colour is a world away from the harsh, dyed blooms that seem to predominate in the shops.

above left
Sunflower
Encourage birds to visit your garden by hanging out dried sunflower heads.

above
Artichokes and lavender
Dry flowers away from direct light to retain their colour.

right

Dried poppy heads

Poppy flowers cannot be dried as they drop their petals, but the seedheads dry well.

above

Drying rack at Hancock village

Racks specifically designed for herb-drying at Hancock Shaker village.

opposite

Lavender ring

A wire frame which has been covered with lavender flowers is both decorative and aromatic.

Drying flowers successfully

A CERTAIN AMOUNT *of experimentation is necessary when you first start to dry flowers. Some*

such as poppy heads and lavender are incredibly easy, while others such as peonies and roses require

a bit more attention for good results.

FLOWERS SHOULD be picked early in the day after the dew has evaporated in fine, dry weather. How long a flower takes to dry depends on its moisture content – papery flowers dry quickly, fleshy flowers are much slower. Most can be dried successfully in a warm, dry spot such as above a central heating boiler or in an airing cupboard, but avoid anywhere humid, such as a bathroom, as the flowers will rot rather than dry. Once the flowers are fully dry, they must be stored in the dark in a dry place to remain in good condition.

LAVENDER *Lavandula*

Pick lavender before the florets are fully opened and bunch with rubber bands, which will tighten as the stems dry and shrink. Dry lavender in a cool, airy position such as hanging from the rafters of the shed or in a hallway, well away from direct light.

PEONY *Paeonia*

Pick peonies when fully open. Hang singly in a warm dry place away from direct light. When they are dry to the touch, put the flowers in a very low oven for four hours to ensure that the centre of the flower has dried through. Store in boxes packed between layers of tissue paper to prevent the flowers being crushed.

POPPY *Papaver*

Poppy heads can be left to ripen on the plant or picked when the petals have dropped. Hang in bunches to dry in a warm, dry position.

ROSE *Rosa*

Pick roses when they are open, but not full-blown. Remove the lower leaves and any thorns and gather into loose bunches. Hang bunches upside down in a warm, dry position, away from direct light. To give dried roses a full-blown appearance hold each rose over a steaming kettle. The petals will soften and can then be gently teased out with a toothpick. As they dry out again the petals will stiffen once more.

MAKING A LAVENDER HEART

Wire, bent into a heart shape,

has been covered with dried lavender flowers

to make a simple decoration. Any other dried flower

or even a herb such as sage could be

used equally effectively.

Materials

approximately 1m (3ft) medium gauge
plastic-covered garden wire

florist's tape · green garden twine · dried lavender

Method

1. Bend the wire into a heart shape and tape the join firmly with florist's tape.

2. Use the twine to bind together 4 or 5 lavender heads to make a small bunch with stems about 5cm (2in) long. You will need approximately 35 of these.

3. Bind two bunches of lavender flowers onto the bottom of the heart so that the flower heads butt up against one another and cover the point.

4. Starting at the top of the heart, bind a bunch of lavender firmly onto the wire frame with the flower heads pointing in towards the centre of the heart.

5. Cover the stems with another bunch of lavender and bind into position. Continue to do this until you have completed one side of the heart and then repeat the process down the other side.

Flowers for Cutting

'IN ORDER THAT WE MIGHT not be tempted to fasten a rose upon a dress or to put it into water to keep, the rule was that the flower should be plucked with no stem at all.'

SISTER MARCIA BULLARD

ASTRANTIA MAJOR   DIANTHUS BARBATUS – SWEET WILLIAM   LATHYRUS ODORATUS 'MATUCANA' – SWEET PEA   ROSA PEGASUS – ROSE

I AM GLAD THAT SISTER MARCIA lived long enough to experience a less restrictive Shaker life where she could enjoy flowers without fear of endangering her soul. She must have taken particular pleasure in a simple bunch of roses picked from the garden, given the earlier prohibitions. Although then never used as cut flowers, roses were an important crop for the early Shakers. The picked petals were most commonly used to make rosewater, which was used for culinary and medicinal purposes.

ROSE OIL

To get the oil of Roses, *Take a large jar and fill it (with) clean flowers of roses. Cover them with pure water and set it in the sun in the day time and take in at night for 7 days when the oil will float on the top. Take this off with some cotton tied on a stick and squeeze in a phyal and stop it up close.*

A SHAKER RECIPE BOOK 1859

(This method yields minute amounts of oil unless done on a vast scale.)

A PERENNIAL CUTTING GARDEN

Planting this type of border solely with flowers that appear in Shaker records would be somewhat limiting, so I have taken some liberties and included modern varieties and cultivars, e.g. the roses are repeat flowering rather than the once flowering varieties that the Shakers grew. As I have said before, this book is not an exercise in historical accuracy and I draw encouragement from the fact that with their love of innovation and progress, the Shakers always readily embraced the new. I have also included the opium poppy *papaver somniferum*, which is an annual, and the biennial foxglove *digitalis purpurea* because they will seed readily in among the perennials.

SOIL PREPARATION

Prepare the soil in Autumn for long-term planting. Clear the ground and dig carefully removing any perennial weeds. Work in well-rotted manure or compost mixed with bonemeal. Heavy soils will benefit from the addition of coarse grit.

PERENNIAL BORDER WITH FLOWERS SUITABLE FOR CUTTING

KEY

1. Rose – *Rosa* 'New Dawn' (*blush pink*)

2. Foxglove – *Digitalis purpurea* (*pink/purple*)

3. *Verbena bonariensis* (*purple*)

4. *Anemone japonica* (*pink/white*)

5. Rose – *Rosa* 'Climbing Iceberg' (*white*)

6. Bronze fennel – *Foeniculum vulgare* (*bronze*)

7. Peony – *Paeonia* 'Sarah Bernhardt' (*pink*)

8. Poppy – *Papaver somniferum* 'Pink Chiffon' (*pink*)

9. *Phlox maculata* 'Eva Callum' (*deep pink*)

10. *Phlox maculata* 'Omega' (*white with pink eye*)

11. Rose – *Rosa* 'Perle d'Or' (*apricot*)

12. *Penstemon* 'Garnet' (*red*)

13. *Tanacetum coccineum* 'Brenda' (*hot pink*)

14. Lavender – *Lavandula* 'Hidcote' (*purple*)

15. *Sedum spectabile* (*rose pink*)

16. *Artemisia abrotanum* (*silver grey*)

17. *Astrantia major rubra* (*red*)

18. *Alchemilla mollis* (*lime green*)

19. *Dianthus* 'Doris' (*pink*)

20. *Anthemis cupaniana* (*white*)

21. *Achillea millefolium* 'Paprika' (*orange/pink*)

CROCOSMIA MASONIORUM

SOLANUM JASMINOIDES ALBUM

PENSTEMON 'GARNET'

DIANTHUS 'MRS SINKINS'

left

Old pewter

The bright colours of sweet peas and purple flowered verbena bonariensis look especially vibrant against the dull silver-grey of old pewter.

below

Rich colours

Flowers from the garden can combine blooms which would seldom be seen together in a bunch from the florist – here shades of yarrow mix with vivid geraniums.

above

Conditioning

All cut flowers need to be stood in deep water in a cool place before they are arranged, otherwise their vase life is considerably reduced.

right

Bright posy

There's no need for a fancy vase for this little posy of informal flowers. Pale yellow marguerites and brightly striped tagetes look quite charming in a jam jar placed on a garden table.

Choosing & planting perennials

THERE IS A TEMPTATION *when buying plants to go for the largest specimen, especially if it is covered in flowers, but this is not recommended as the more mature a plant is, the greater will be the stress of transplantation. It is worth remembering that many perennials need to be divided every three years – buying a large plant simply shortens the time before this is necessary.*

BY PLANTING IN AUTUMN you will give the plants an opportunity to root into the surrounding soil at a time when the leaves and flowers are not competing with the roots for available moisture and nutrients. Buy your plants from a reputable nursery that will check your selection and advise you if any are unsuitable for your climate zone and suggest alternatives. Dormant plants should have a good root system, but the roots should not fill the entire pot or protrude through the base.

Dig a hole that comfortably accommodates the rootball of the plant and check that the soil will be the same level around the stem as it was in the pot. Water each plant before filling in around the rootball with soil and press down firmly to ensure that there are no air pockets between the roots and the surrounding soil. A protective mulch of a composted material will suppress weeds and protect the plants from the worst of the winter. In spring each year top-dress with fish blood-and-bone and apply a mulch of compost. This will reduce the need for watering.

PLANT SUPPORTS

In the spring the plants will grow rapidly and will soon need supporting if they are to remain upright rather than flopping. Manufactured plant supports are available, but twiggy branches look much nicer. Push the branches around the plants when the growth is about 15cm (6in) high. As the plants grow they will conceal the twigs but remain upright in all but the most extreme weather.

PICKING & CONDITIONING FLOWERS

Flowers should be picked in the cool of the day, preferably in the morning. As soon as they have been cut stand them, preferably in the dark, in deep, cool, but not cold water for at least four hours, preferably overnight. This is called conditioning – it ensures that they last well and do not flop in the vase. When arranging the flowers remove all foliage that would be below water level. The addition of a teaspoon each of sugar, bleach and vinegar will reduce bacteria in the water and further prolong the flowers' vase life.

DIVIDING PLANTS

After three years some perennials, including phlox, tanacetum and achillea, will need dividing to ensure plenty of flowers. This should be done in late autumn or early spring. Dig up the entire plant and remove clumps from the outside of the plant. These can be replanted or potted up to give to friends. The centre of the plant should be discarded.

above

Auricula

To be certain of healthy free-flowering plants, especially specialist ones like auricula, select them from a reputable nursery and be guided by advice on which plants will suit the conditions in your garden.

Annual Flower Patch

FEW ANNUAL FLOWERS *are listed as growing in early Shaker gardens, although they do appear in later seed catalogues. The annuals that were grown would have been planted in straight rows, and the flowers left to set seed, which was packaged and sold to 'the World'. There must have been many occasions of temptation for the Shakers working among those flowers – the heady fragrance and delicate beauty of sweet peas, the dazzling brilliance of zinnias and the musky scent of petunias are all hard to ignore and must have caused a few spiritual struggles as the Shakers tried to resist the seductive beauty of the flowers.*

ANNUAL POSY

Annual-flowering plants are amazingly productive. There will be plenty of flowers for the home, and sufficient to make delightful posies to give to friends and relatives.

opposite

Planting plan

An annual flower patch can be simply planted in straight rows as the Shakers would have done, but this patchwork layout with a path zig-zagging through is more appealing to modern tastes.

FORTUNATELY, LIKE THE LATER SHAKERS, we can enjoy growing flowers without risking our spiritual well-being. If your garden is large enough, it is worthwhile establishing an annual flower patch, or devoting a corner of the vegetable garden to flowers. Annuals can be tricky in the perennial border where they must compete for space with the other plants and it is sometimes difficult to differentiate between the young flower seedlings and weeds. On the other hand an area devoted to annual flowers can be prepared specifically for them and will provide ideal growing conditions.

Good soil preparation is always important especially for annuals, which are sown directly where they will flower. They do best in friable soil enriched with compost and worked down to a fine tilth. If possible, cover the prepared soil with horticultural

ANNUAL FLOWER PATCH

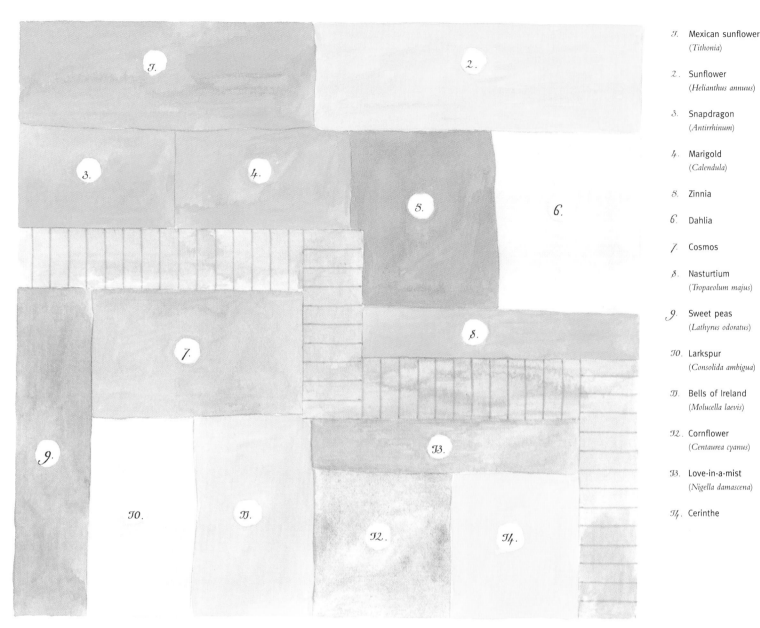

1. Mexican sunflower
   (*Tithonia*)

2. Sunflower
   (*Helianthus annuus*)

3. Snapdragon
   (*Antirrhinum*)

4. Marigold
   (*Calendula*)

5. Zinnia

6. Dahlia

7. Cosmos

8. Nasturtium
   (*Tropaeolum majus*)

9. Sweet peas
   (*Lathyrus odoratus*)

10. Larkspur
    (*Consolida ambigua*)

11. Bells of Ireland
    (*Molucella laevis*)

12. Cornflower
    (*Centaurea cyanus*)

13. Love-in-a-mist
    (*Nigella damascena*)

14. Cerinthe

fleece and leave the patch for two or three weeks before sowing seeds. This will allow weeds to germinate – they can then be hoed out and removed before sowing takes place.

In areas where the growing season is very short, it may be necessary to sow the seeds under cover and then pot the seedlings on, before planting outdoors once the soil has warmed sufficiently. Whether sown under cover or outdoors, it is essential that the seedlings are thinned to the recommended rate or you will end up with lots of puny plants rather than the colourful display you hoped for. As *The Gardener's Manual* instructs: 'Leaving plants too thick is a prevalent error, and one to which gardeners are very liable.'

ESCHSCHOLZIA — CALIFORNIA POPPY   TITHONIA ROTUNDIFOLIA   NIGELLA DAMASCENA — LOVE-IN-A-MIST

Recommended annuals

MY PLAN FOR AN ANNUAL FLOWER PATCH *is a compromise between the Shaker love of order and symmetry and the modern preference for a less rigid approach. Rather than planting the flowers in straight rows I have created a patchwork of colour, more suited to contemporary tastes, with the strong, hot colours on one side of the plank path, and softer, cooler colours on the other side.*

Both the tithonia and the sunflowers are tall-growing plants and are best grown against a wall or fence, while the sweet peas need some sort of framework to climb over. The other plants benefit from twiggy support to prevent them flopping over as they grow. An annual flower garden should be in a sheltered, sunny position with well-drained soil enriched with compost and top-dressed with fish, blood and bone. All these flowers are good for cutting and can supplement those from the cutting garden.

SNAPDRAGON *Antirrhinum majus*

The snapdragon is an easy-to-grow, old-fashioned flower available in every colour from snow-white to deep reddish-black and in a range of heights. Look for varieties that are rust resistant. Sow outdoors in late spring or earlier under glass. When the plants are 15cm (6in) tall pinch out the growing tips to encourage bushy plants. Dead-head regularly to encourage the formation of more flowers.

POT MARIGOLD *Calendula officinalis*

One of the easiest of all annual flowers. Tall varieties such as 'Geisha Girl' and 'Kablouna' series, which reach a height of 60cm (24in), are ideal for cutting. Sow thinly where they are to flower in spring or

autumn in mild areas. Dead-head regularly. Seed can be saved for next year.

CORNFLOWER *Centaurea cyanus*

Another easy annual. Most cornflower seed is sold in packets of mixed colours that range from white through pink and blue to deep burgundy. I prefer to grow the pure blue varieties as the impact of a solid block of colour is much greater. Sow where they are to flower — twiggy support will stop their tendency to flop all over the place.

Cerinthe major

This is a fairly new introduction that is well worth growing for its stunning blue-green leaves and

purple-blue flowering bracts which positively glow with colour in the evening light. It germinates readily and grows quickly. Pinch out growing tips to encourage a bushy plant. Save seed for next year.

LARKSPUR *Consolida ambigua*

The feathery foliage and pastel flowers of larkspur make it an ideal candidate for the annual flower garden, although it will need to be supported by twigs to look its best. Sow seed where it is to flower in spring, or autumn in warmer zones.

COSMOS DAISY *Cosmos bippinatus*

Every annual garden should have a group of cosmos daisies. It is utterly reliable and will flower

CENTAUREA CYANUS – CORNFLOWER

TAGETES 'HARLEQUIN'

HELIANTHUS ANNUUS – SUNFLOWER

right up to the first frosts. Sow under glass in early spring or in situ in spring or autumn depending on your climate. Pinch out the growing tip when plants are 15cm (6in) tall. Seed can be saved.

DAHLIA

Dahlias are not strictly annuals, but they do need lifting annually as the tubers are not frost-hardy. Although they are more labour intensive than the other flowers they are worth the effort for their glorious blooms. Tubers can be sprouted under glass or planted out once all danger of frost is past. Plants will benefit from staking. 'Bishop of Llandaff' with bronze foliage and bright red flowers is my favourite.

CALIFORNIA POPPY *Eschscholzia*

The California poppy grows in light, sandy soils and once it is established it will self-seed freely.

SUNFLOWER *Helianthus annuus*

Sunflowers used to be yellow and grow very tall. Modern plant breeding has produced many new colours from palest cream to deep ruby red, and plants that are shorter and bushier – more suited to the average garden. Sow seeds in pairs where they are to flower. When they germinate remove one seedling and leave the other to grow. Plants will

benefit from staking. Save some seed and hang up the remaining seedheads for the birds.

SWEET PEA *Lathyrus odoratus*

Sweet peas are a must for the annual garden. They do best in deeply cultivated, rich soil topped-dressed with lime. Soak seed before sowing in pots in early spring and plant out in late spring. Pinch out the growing tips when plants are 10cm (4in) high. Sweet peas need supports up which they can climb – put these in position before planting to avoid damaging the root systems. For continuous flowering do not allow any flowers to set seed. In the autumn cut down dead stems and foliage, but leave roots in the soil to release nitrogen.

BELLS OF IRELAND *Molucella leavis*

The lime green spires of Molucella are a foil for all the flowers in the garden. Sow thinly under glass in early spring or outdoors in late spring. Supporting twigs will ensure the spires grow straight.

LOVE-IN-A-MIST *Nigella damascena*

The soft, hazy blue of Love-in-a-mist makes it a must for the annual garden. Sow outdoors in early autumn or late spring depending on your climate. Dead-head the plants regularly to encourage continuous flowering.

MEXICAN SUNFLOWER *Tithonia*

The intense orange flowers will brighten the flower patch from mid-summer onwards. Best sown under glass in early spring and planted out after the last frost. Provide twiggy support. Dead-head regularly. Seed can be saved for next year.

NASTURTIUM *Tropaeolum majus*

Another very easy annual. Choose bush varieties, rather than trailing nasturtiums, for the annual flower patch or they will quickly smother their neighbours. Watch out for caterpillar infestation later in the summer – pick off the affected leaves, or in extreme cases it may be wise to pull up the entire plant. Self-seeds readily.

Tagetes

Tagetes daisies can be sown outdoors in late spring or earlier under glass. When sown outdoors they should be thinned early to ensure bushy plants, which can also be encouraged by pinching out the growing tips once the plants have two sets of leaves.

Zinnia

Brilliantly colourful flowers which do best in free-draining soil. For best results, sow under glass in spring and plant out after the last frosts. Dead-head regularly.

Edible flowers

MAKE A STRONG *decoction of rose flowers sweetened very sweet*

with white sugar, add a little sulfuric acid enough to make sharp, look red, and taste well.

RECIPE FOR ROSE SYRUP MADE AT CANTERBURY VILLAGE *(not recommended)*

By THE END of the nineteenth century many of the early strictures on growing flowers that were not demonstrably useful had disappeared, but until that time, edible flowers must have been a welcome addition to the medicinal flowers that the Shaker gardeners were allowed to grow. The only edible flower listed in *The Gardener's Manual* is the nasturtium; it was chiefly valued for its caper-like berries, which were pickled in spicy vinegar, although a surviving Shaker recipe for green bean salad uses the flowers and leaves as well as the berries to give the salad a peppery kick.

Today, with a few exceptions, edible flowers are generally added to food for their decorative qualities rather than their taste. Supermarkets sell edible flowers for garnishing summer salads and smart restaurants decorate plates so lavishly there often seems to be more decoration than nourishment. The Shakers would not have approved of this, but the inclusion of a few freshly picked flowers to a home grown salad celebrates the bounty of the garden.

With the exception of the elderflowers that grow in an adjoining hedgerow, all the other edible flowers are grown in my Shaker garden where I can be sure that they have not been contaminated by pesticides or other harmful chemicals. Do not eat any flowers unless you are sure they come from a safe source.

opposite

Salad bowl

Marigold petals, nasturtium, borage and sage flowers add colour and piquant flavour to a summer salad.

left

Edible flowers

The blue star-shaped flowers of the borage plant have a delicate cucumber flavour.

BORAGE

ROSE PETALS

Tasty flowers

BORAGE *Borago officinalis*

The sky blue flowers of borage have a delicious cucumber fragrance, which is delicious added to green salads, fruit salads, iced teas and cordials. The young leaves have a similar flavour, but quickly develop prickly hairs, so they should be eaten very young or not at all.

Once you have successfully grown borage in your garden, you need have no fear for its future as this is a plant that self-seeds very readily. Borage is an annual plant and the seeds can be sown anytime from early spring onwards in sunny well-drained soil. It will flower in eight weeks and keep flowering until the first frosts when it will quickly blacken and die. In the following seasons as the seedlings appear all over the garden, transplant those you wish to keep and ruthlessly remove the rest or they will take over.

Honey bees love borage flowers and the plant is also said to have a beneficial effect on the growth of strawberry plants.

POT MARIGOLD *Calendula officinalis*

Marigold petals can be used to add colour to salads. They should be used in moderation as their flavour is quite strong. In the past it was known as 'poor man's saffron' and was added to soups and stews. Sow in open ground in the autumn or spring depending on your climate. It will self-seed readily.

COURGETTE (ZUCCHINI) FLOWER

The productivity of a single courgette plant can sometimes overwhelm one's capacity to eat them. One solution is to pick them early, when the flower is fully open and the courgette is little more than finger size. After removing the stem and calyx, the flowers can be shredded into a salad, dipped in tempura batter and deep fried, or chopped, cooked briefly in butter and added to an omelette.

For instructions on how to grow courgettes, see page 117.

NASTURTIUM *Tropaeolum majus*

This is an annual plant, a native of Peru, and is much cultivated for the berries, which if gathered while green and pickled in vinegar, make a good substitute for capers. Sow as early as the season will admit, in drills an inch deep. The plants should be supported from the ground by bushy sticks, or otherwise, in order to have them do well and produce a plentiful crop of good fruit.

THE GARDENER'S MANUAL

Nasturtiums will produce a higher proportion of flowers when grown in poor soil.

PICKLING NASTURTIUM BERRIES

– must be gathered when they have just attained their full size, and while they are green, plump, and tender. Spice the vinegar, and pour it on while hot.

THE GARDENER'S MANUAL

ROSE *Rosa*

Rose petals can be frosted to decorate a cake, used as a filling for delicate sandwiches or made into rose-petal jam. Personally I find the flavour a bit too perfumed for my liking and prefer to enjoy my roses in a vase!

SAGE *Salvia officinalis*

Looking around the Shaker garden to check if I had made a note of all the edible flowers growing in it, I noticed that some of the sage plants were in flower. Feeling experimental I pulled one of the flowers off its stem and tasted it. It was delicious – a delicate sage flavour with a touch of sweetness. Use the flowers in salads, pasta dishes or omelettes, but be sure to include only the blue petals or the flavour will be less subtle.

To encourage sage to flower all summer be sure to trim off the heads as soon as the flowers begin to fade and die. For full cultivation notes, see page 77.

NASTURTIUM (AND BELOW)

DOUBLE NASTURTIUM

ELDERFLOWER

RECIPE

ELDERFLOWER CORDIAL

Ingredients

1.5 litres (2 ¹/₂ pints) boiling water

1.5kg (3lbs) sugar

25 elderflower heads, washed and drained

2 unwaxed organic, sliced lemons

50g (2oz) citric acid

Method

Dissolve sugar in the boiling water and leave to cool. Stir in the citric acid and add elderflowers and sliced lemons. Cover and leave for three days, stirring occasionally. Strain and pour into clean, sterilized bottles and then seal. Store in a cool place – it will keep indefinitely. Dilute to taste with still or sparkling mineral water.

ELDERFLOWER *Sambucus nigra*

It is not normally necessary to cultivate elderflowers as they grow wild by roadsides and in hedgerows. The lacy white flower heads appear in late spring and early summer. Although the elder plant has a rank smell, the flavour of the flowers is extremely delicate. They are traditionally used to make a refreshing cordial.

Birds, Bees & Butterflies

LIKE ALL GOOD GARDENERS, *the Shakers would have been familiar with the local birds as well as bees and butterflies, and would have known which were welcome visitors in the garden and which were not. In addition, with their careful observation and note-taking, they are sure to have known which plants should be grown to attract beneficial insects and other pollinators. Each community had beehives in their orchards to ensure pollination of the blossom and provide delicious honey for the table.*

ALTHOUGH IT MAY NOT BE PRACTICAL to have one or more beehives in the garden (it certainly isn't in mine), by growing the right plants your garden will soon be abuzz with bees, butterflies and hoverflies. My Shaker garden is too small to accommodate these flowers alongside the vegetables, so I have planted them just outside

the fence so that the garden can benefit from their presence without losing precious growing space. Also growing outside the Shaker garden are 'sacrifice' plants where butterflies can lay their eggs and ensure future generations. These include asters, daisies, honeysuckle, fennel and nettles. Within the Shaker garden the presence of nasturtiums and *tagetes* encourages beneficial hoverflies.

Elsewhere in the garden a bramble patch and berry-bearing shrubs and trees attract the birds as do the seedheads of grasses and flowers that are left untrimmed until the spring. Bird feeders hang in the trees to provide extra winter food.

left

Butterfly

A butterfly feeds on the nectar of a Verbena bonariensus. *Butterflies will only visit plants growing in full sun.*

opposite

Bee

*By planting flowers which attract bees, such as this globe thistle (*Echinops ritro*) the gardener ensures that the essential process of pollination takes place.*

VERBENA BONARIENSIS

BUDDLEIA DAVIDII

Recommended plants

BENEFICIAL INSECTS AND BIRDS are very specific about the plants that they do and do not like. Flowers that look wonderful to the human eye sometimes have little or no appeal to them, while drab or insignificant plants may act like magnets. The following selection aims to balance the requirements of the gardener with those of the birds, bees and butterflies.

BUTTERFLY WEED *Asclepia tuberosa*
The brilliant orange flowers of this tuberous perennial are irresistible to butterflies. Plant in full sun, in well-drained soil. Dead-heading will extend the flowering season but be careful as the milky sap can irritate the skin.

BUTTERFLY BUSH *Buddleia davidii*
When buddleia is in full flower it is a magnet for butterflies of every sort and each flower spike is covered with fluttering wings as they feed on the nectar. It is a rapid growing shrub that can easily reach 2m (6ft) in a season. Leave it unpruned overwinter and then cut back to 20cm (6in) in early spring. Although generally hardy, it should be grown as an annual in the coldest zones.

GLOBE THISTLE *Echinops retro*
A prickly customer with spherical blue thistle-like flowers, it does best in poor soil. Bees and hoverflies visit it continuously when it is in full bloom. It is best cut back hard as soon as the flowers start to fade.

SUNFLOWER *Helianthus annuus*
A patch of sunflowers will prove popular with the insects when they are in flower and then provide winter food for the birds once they set seed. The shorter varieties now available are easier to accommodate in smaller gardens, although, space permitting, the traditional sunflower is a magnificent sight. Leave the seedheads to ripen on the plant. In the autumn cut them off with a short length of stem and hang them upside down to complete the ripening process. During the winter hang the seedheads outdoors and enjoy watching the birds feeding from them.

COMMON LAVENDER *Lavandula angustifolia*
Bees love lavender and visit it constantly when it is in full flower. It is best used to line a path where its scent can be fully appreciated and it is easy to observe the bees at work. Lavender must be grown in very free-draining soil in full sun. In regions where it is not hardy it can be grown in pots, which

can be given protection over winter. To keep a nice bushy look to the plants, they should be cut back to a rounded shape after flowering. The Shakers harvested lavender to make lavender water, pot pourri and lavender bags that they sold to 'the World'.

BERGAMOT OR BEE BALM *Monarda didyma*
Grown by the Shakers for Oswego tea and medicinal purposes, as its common name Bee Balm indicates, this is another plant that is much loved by bees. For full cultivation instructions, see page 80.

SWEET MARJORAM *Origanum vulgare*
Sweet marjoram was one of the culinary herbs cultivated by the Shakers. Its pink flowers attract bees. For cultivation instructions, see page 76.

ICE PLANT *Sedum spectabile*
The ice plant is an autumn flowering plant that is guaranteed to attract butterflies to the garden. The broad, flat heads of starry pink flowers are held above fleshy green leaves. Sedums do best in full

ASCLEPIA TUBEROSA   HELIANTHUS ANNUUS   SEDUM SPECTABILE

sun, in fertile, well-drained soil and are hardy to -5°C. Once established they divide easily to propagate new plants.

CREEPING THYME   *Thymus serpyllum*

This was the variety of thyme favoured by the Shakers who naturalised it in their orchards. It is ideal for planting between bricks or paving slabs on a pathway, or planted in a wall where this prostrate thyme, with flowers that vary from white to deep red, can spread without competition from other plants. It should be planted into very free-draining soil.

Verbena bonariensis

An unusual tall verbena, normally grown as an annual although it can survive the winter in milder regions. The purple flowers are carried at the top of unobtrusive stems, which allows a clear view of the surrounding plants and gives the impression of a cloud of purple flowers hovering above the border. The flowers provide perfect landing platforms for butterflies.

'You take a world of pains ' *I said*

'Ah, Brother Hepworth, *thee sees*

we love *our* garden '

Hepworth Dixon – *an English visitor*

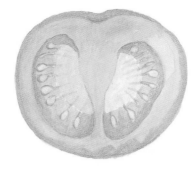

lycopersicon lycopersicon

vegetables

'Here let it be stated, *once and for all, that all culinary vegetables do best upon a good rich soil; therefore let your land, if not naturally quite rich, be plentifully manured; and even if the land be quite fertile, if it has been used much, a slight manuring will be beneficial.'*

THE GARDENER'S MANUAL

THE SHAKERS LIVED AT A TIME when all gardening was organic and there were no quick solutions or easy remedies to replace good husbandry. Then as now there were good gardeners and not-so-good gardeners, and the Shakers devised *The Gardener's Manual* to help what they referred to as 'the common classes, those to whom a garden is of the most real value' become good gardeners and provide wholesome food for their families. They knew that the key to successful crops was good soil management and their Manual said of gardens of the time that 'Very many are deficient in the variety of vegetables cultivated; and a majority not properly prepared before stocking with seeds and plants, and but poorly cultivated when stocked.'

In modern terms *The Gardener's Manual* was a marketing tool, so the comment about the deficiency in vegetable varieties would have been made with increased seed sales in mind. That aside, the Manual is filled with valuable advice and information. The Shaker's reputation for the quality of their produce was unsurpassed and there is no doubt that gardeners in 'the World' would have been eager to learn their ways, at a time when there was little help for the gardener.

Today we are gardening organically from choice as we see the drive for ever-cheaper food causing one health scare after another. More and more of us buy organic food, and those of us who have the space are growing our own vegetables. If the Shaker communities of the past were still around today, you can be certain that we would be flocking to their stalls at farmers' markets to buy the very best produce that they would have been enthusiastically selling to 'the World'.

The only advice in *The Gardener's Manual* that I did not follow was on making and managing a hot-bed. These were much used by the Shakers for the germinating and growing of early crops. As the Manual says of hot beds, 'their management is quite particular, and requires you to be thoughtful and regular; but this is only promoting a good habit, and if you were inclined to forgetfulness, would almost justify keeping one expressly for that purpose.' Almost – but not quite – my electric propagator is a 20th century invention that would surely have been welcomed by the ever innovative Shakers.

opposite

Shaker onions

Onions were raised for their seed which was a major cash crop for some of the communities. They were also an important ingredient in Shaker cookery and this archive photograph shows that a good crop was considered worth recording.

THE PLANTED SHAKER GARDEN

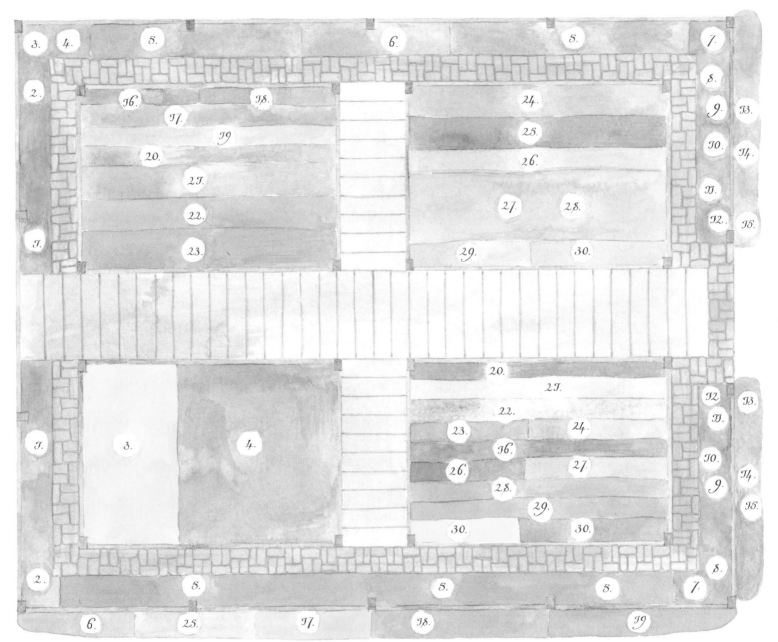

Key for top half of garden

1.	Runner beans	*11.*	Echinacea	*21.*	Dwarf French beans
2.	Gem squash	*12.*	Roman chamomile	*22.*	Marigolds
3.	Lovage	*13.*	Rosemary	*23.*	Strawberries
4.	Sweet peas	*14.*	Lavender	*24.*	Mange tout *(sugar snaps)*
5.	Thornless blackberry	*15.*	Thyme	*25.*	Aubergines *(eggplant)*
6.	Comfrey	*16.*	Spinach	*26.*	Oak leaf lettuce
7.	Globe artichoke	*17.*	Peas	*27.*	Courgette *(zucchini)*
8.	Sorrel	*18.*	Rocket	*28.*	Acorn squash
9.	German chamomile	*19.*	Lettuce 'Little Gem'	*29.*	Red sage
10.	Flat parsley	*20.*	Ruby chard	*30.*	Basil

Key for lower half of garden

1.	Runner beans	*11.*	Echinacea	*21.*	Carrots
2.	Sunflowers	*12.*	Roman chamomile	*22.*	Onions
3.	Sweetcorn	*13.*	Rosemary	*23.*	Beetroot
4.	Potatoes	*14.*	Lavender	*24.*	Golden beet
5.	Tomatoes	*15.*	Thyme	*25.*	Fennel
6.	Angelica	*16.*	Spinach	*26.*	Parsnips
7.	Globe artichoke	*17.*	Rudbeckia	*27.*	Radishes
8.	Red orach	*18.*	Bergamot	*28.*	Cornflowers
9.	Peppers	*19.*	Feverfew	*29.*	Turnips
10.	Nasturtiums	*20.*	Tagetes/sage	*30.*	Curly parsley

Root Vegetables

BEETS AND CARROTS SHOULD BE GATHERED *before hard frosts in the Fall, the tops removed and the roots packed away in sand in a cool cellar. A good method of preserving Carrots fresh through the Winter is to lay them in a circular pattern on the floor of the cellar, with the roots in the centre and heads outward; cover the first course with sand; then lay another course upon them, and cover with sand as before, and so on until all are packed and covered. The sand for Carrots should be very dry or they will rot; for Beets it may be moist, but not wet.*

THE GARDENER'S MANUAL

BECAUSE THEY STORE SO well, root vegetables were important to the Shakers. They grew several varieties of carrot and beetroot, winter and summer radishes, parsnips, salsify, turnips and rutabaga. Their harvested root vegetables were enormous by today's standards, but the higher starch content ensured that they stored well and provided important carbohydrate for the hungry Shakers.

BEETROOT

Sow very early, in drills 18 inches apart and 1 deep. Thin the first time to 4 inches, the last to 8.

THE GARDENER'S MANUAL

Beetroot seeds germinate better if the seeds are put into a fine sieve and rinsed under running water. With the modern taste for smaller vegetables it is not necessary to do a second thinning, and they can be grown even closer together where space is limited. Successional sowings will provide regular pickings of beetroot from late spring through to the autumn when the maincrop is ready.

PICKLED BEETROOT

Boil them, scrape off the skin, and soak them in vinegar 24 hours, or till wanted for use. When thus prepared they form an excellent substitute for pickled cucumbers. Winter stored beetroot are also delicious when they are baked in their skins.

THE GARDENER'S MANUAL

CARROTS

Instructions on growing carrots are very brief indeed in *The Gardener's Manual* – 'Sow the same as beets, and thin to 4 inches.' *The Gardener's Manual* lists three varieties: Long Orange, Early Horn and Altringham. Carrots do best on light soil enriched with well-rotted manure or compost. On heavy soils it is better to

above

Beetroot

Maincrop beetroot can be stored in damp sand for the winter. Their leaves should be twisted off rather than cut to prevent them 'bleeding'.

left

Carrots

A barrel of maincrop carrots is prepared for winter storage. Layers of the carrots are arranged in a radiating pattern and then covered with sand.

opposite

Root vegetables

Today we like to eat our vegetables as young and tender as possible, either raw or lightly cooked. Things were very different for the Shakers who grew vast vegetables – this was not just to ensure that they had plenty of food for the winter – the longer a plant was left to grow the more the sugars were converted to starch which was nutritionally more important for the hard-working Shakers..

plant them in raised beds or ridges. Acid soils should have a dressing of lime before sowing. Water carrots regularly to prevent them becoming tough and woody. Where carrot root fly damage is a problem it can be prevented by erecting a low screen around the carrots or protecting them with horticultural fleece – the root fly travels just above ground level and the screen will deflect it away from the carrots. Carrots are best pulled in late autumn and stored – left in the garden they will attract slugs.

PARSNIPS

Cultivate as Carrots. In November dig enough for winter use, and put in the cellar; let the rest stand in the ground till spring.

THE GARDENER'S MANUAL.

Parsnips do best in soil enriched with compost and dressed with lime (unless it is already alkaline). The flavour of the parsnip is improved by exposure to frost, so it is preferable not to dig any before the first frost of the season, but they will need lifting before the ground gets too hard to work. Parsnip seed is very slow to germinate, especially if the ground is cold. Sow 2 or 3 seeds at 15cm (6in) intervals in late spring in a shallow drill and inter-sow with quick growing radish to mark the row. When the parsnips have germinated, thin to the strongest seedling in each group. Regular watering will prevent the roots cracking.

SALSIFY

This vegetable, in appearance, resembles a small parsnip; it is raised annually from the seed, and may be cultivated in the same manner as parsnips or carrots, and is as easily raised. It is a vegetable highly esteemed by those best acquainted with it. It is very hardy, and may stand in the ground through the winter, if you wish.

THE GARDENER'S MANUAL.

This delicious vegetable deserves to be more popular. Peeled and steamed it can be eaten on its own or it can be chopped raw and added to soups and stews. To prevent the roots forking it is essential that it is grown in deep, well-cultivated soil, and that any compost or manure that is added is well-rotted.

TURNIP

Sow and cultivate the same as Onions, in the Garden.

THE GARDENER'S MANUAL.

This is rather a strange comparison as turnips and onions are very different vegetables, although the recommended spacing of 'drills, 16 inches apart and half an inch deep' seems fair enough. Turnips germinate and grow readily in limed and manured soil. Thin plants to 5cm (2in) apart and pick them young to taste them at their best. Flea beetle can be a problem, riddling the leaves with holes. When the plants are about 5cm (2in) high, run a card smeared with Vaseline along the row – the beetles will jump off the plants and stick to the card! Repeat as necessary.

Squashes & Pumpkins

SQUASHES REQUIRE *to be treated much after the manner of melons and cucumbers. The Sweet Potato Squash and Winter Crook-neck, as they produce running vines, require to be planted in hills at the distance of six or eight feet. The Summer Crook-neck and the Summer Scollep, being what are called bush Squashes, as they have no running vines, may be planted in hills about four feet apart each way.*

THE GARDENER'S MANUAL

above left

Hancock pumpkins

Part of the autumn harvest of pumpkins is laid out on the grass in the garden in front of the Round Barn at the Hancock Shaker Village.

SHAKER SEED CATALOGUES list at least six varieties of squash that they grew, as well as a number of pumpkins such as Connecticut Field and Common Field. These vegetables were originally grown by the Native Americans, but soon became popular with the settlers. Because these early varieties of pumpkin did not store well for long, the Shakers peeled, dried and sliced them and made 'pumpkin flour'.

As the extract from *The Gardener's Manual* explains, there are two types of plant in this family, those with running vines and the bush varieties. Space will often require that the bush varieties are chosen, although it is worth remembering that some of the trailing

above

Squashes

Provided they are fully ripened, squashes can be stored in an open basket (centre). A larger container is needed for pumpkins — such as a slatted wooden box (right).

plants that bear small fruit can be trained over supports. In my Shaker garden I grew bush courgettes (zucchini), what I thought were bush acorn squash (they sent out rampant vines) and trailing gem squash. Fortunately the acorn squash grew at the edge of a raised bed and I was able to guide its vines onto the path and under the fence where it was free to run wild without overwhelming its neighbours.

The gem squash was easier to control with its globe-shaped fruit that grow to around 15cm (6in) in diameter. I planted the young plants in the narrow bed at the north end of the garden and as the vines grew I wound the tendrils in and out along the top of the picket fence so that, as they formed, the squashes hung down from the vine like large green Christmas baubles. Useful beauty at its best, and wonderfully easy to pick.

above

Pumpkins

If you wish to store pumpkins through the winter be sure to choose a variety which has good keeping qualities or you will need to cook them for freezing or bottling.

right

Basket

*Acorn squash, courgettes
and gem squash were all
grown in my Shaker
garden.*

opposite

Courgette flower

*The courgette plant is a
wonder to behold – in
its brief growing season
it achieves an
astonishing rate of
growth, dwarfing most
other plants in the
vegetable garden. Its
golden flowers are both
good to look at and
good to eat and it will
produce a prolific
quantity of courgettes
providing that you pick
them regularly and don't
leave it to produce a
solitary giant.*

All squashes, gourds and pumpkins need to be grown in very rich, moisture retaining soil to ensure that they grow rapidly and without being checked. In the right conditions they are among the fastest growing garden vegetables, but because they are tender they cannot be sown outdoors until all risk of frost is past. Alternatively the seeds can be sown under glass in mid-spring and then transplanted into the garden under cloches or after the last frost. Sow seed in 8cm (3in) pots with two seeds per pot. Once germinated, thin to the strongest seedling and plant out or re-pot into a larger pot as soon as the roots appear through the drainage holes in the base of the pot.

The soil should be prepared by digging in plenty of well-rotted manure or compost and then forming mounds into which you will plant the seeds or the young plants. Scoop out the centre of each mound to create a dip and sow or plant into the centre of it. This will ensure that water sinks down to the roots of the plant rather than running down the sides of the mound, and also helps create a moist micro-climate for the young plant. Once it is growing strongly, a mulch will keep the roots moist between waterings. A regular liquid feed with seaweed or another organic fertiliser is recommended.

Slugs and snails are the major pests and you will probably need to protect the young seedlings from their predations, but once they get going they will grow faster than the slugs or snails can eat them. The Shakers recommend spacing bush varieties 4ft (1.25m) apart and trailing varieties 6-8ft (1.75-2.5m) apart. When grown in rows, bush courgettes (zucchini) can be planted closer together, but bear in mind that two plants will usually produce sufficient, and sometimes too much, for the average family.

Courgettes (zucchini) are best picked young when they are approximately 15-20cm (6-8in) long, or they can be picked even younger if you are going to eat the flowers (see Edible Flowers, pages 98-101). Left unattended, courgettes (zucchini) turn into marrows, which are not very exciting to eat.

Unless you are competing with the neighbours, avoid growing the giant varieties of pumpkins. Choose a variety recommended for flavour rather than size. Leave them to mature on the plant for as long as possible (standing them on a brick or block of wood helps prevent rotting) and then store them in a dry, well-ventilated place to complete the ripening process. Squashes should be treated in the same way.

Potatoes

THESE ARE THE REQUISITE *qualities for a good potato when one is cut in two; there must be a considerable amount of moisture, though not too much; rub the two pieces together and a whiter froth will appear; this signifies the presence of starch, and the more starch, the better the potato.*

THE SHAKER MANIFESTO *(1881)*

RECIPE

POTATO SALAD

Slice thin six or eight medium-sized boiled potatoes; mince fine two silver-skin onions, so as to get the flavour and not detect the onions in pieces; mix parsley and the potatoes with the onions, and season with salt and cayenne pepper. Moisten one-third of a teaspoonful of dried mustard with a teaspoonful of hot water; put the yolk of two eggs in same dish, beat together with an egg-beater until well-mixed, then drip in a sweet oil, beating it all the time until it thickens like a custard, add one and a half teaspoonfuls of vinegar. Put this dressing over the potatoes and mix all together. The dish can be garnished with celery tops and made very pretty.

MARY WHITCHER'S SHAKER HOUSE-KEEPER *(1882)*

AS POTATOES WERE a staple part of their diet, the Shakers grew their potatoes on a field scale rather than as a garden crop and each community would grow several acres of potatoes annually. There is no record of the varieties they grew and potatoes, either as tubers or seed, were not listed in their seed catalogues. Because potatoes were universally grown there is little mention of their cultivation in *The Gardener's Manual* except to recommend their use as a first crop on newly cultivated land – 'As gardening should not be undertaken on turf land just broken up, we shall consider the garden free from turf, and considerably ameliorated, as it should be, by a crop of potatoes.' This is still a recommended practice when establishing a new garden, not only do the potatoes help break up the land, and suppress weeds, but they act as a 'sacrificial' crop that helps identify grassland pests that may be a problem in the garden. For example, substantial nematode damage to the potatoes would indicate that it would be advisable to plant plenty of *tagetes* in the garden the following year.

Potatoes were eaten at every meal in some Shaker communities. In a cookbook published by Frederick Evans, a New Lebanon Shaker, he records that baked or broiled potatoes were eaten at breakfast, and mashed potatoes or boiled rice were supper time staples.

Mary Whitcher's Shaker House-keeper (1882) has a recipe for a delicious potato salad, as appealing to modern tastes as it was then.

left

Potatoes

The chore of washing freshly-dug potatoes is amply rewarded by the flavour and texture of a home grown crop. Dig carefully to avoid damaging any of the tubers.

opposite

Potato flower

Unless you have a large garden you are unlikely to grow all the potatoes you will need for the year, so choose a favourite variety of salad potato or one that is ready really early instead of a main crop variety. Potatoes are ready for digging once the flowers have died and foliage stops growing.

above

Seed potatoes

Seed potatoes have been allowed to 'chit' i.e. sprout. Only two sprouts are left on each tuber, the rest are rubbed off prior to planting.

The potato crop in my Shaker garden was on a very small scale, with the main crop grown elsewhere. Where space is limited it is best to grow early varieties or a really good salad potato to enjoy as a special treat.

It is essential to buy seed potatoes or eyes from a source which has been certified as disease free. Tubers should be bought early in the year and stood in a light position to sprout at a temperature of around 10°C (50°F). Sprouts should be short, bushy and dark green, if they are paler and longer they are too warm. Select the smaller tubers with the fewest sprouts for the best results – one or two is ideal. Eyes are supplied packed in moist vermiculite and only need to be potted up and put in the greenhouse or on a windowsill until it's time to plant them outdoors. Potatoes need a moisture-retentive soil that has been enriched with large quantities of well-rotted manure or compost. If your supply of manure or compost is limited you can restrict the manure to the planting

above left

Digging potatoes

Dig just enough potatoes for a meal and leave the rest in the ground to retain their earthy flavour. When the weather starts to turn cold and wet in autumn you will need to harvest any remaining tubers.

trenches rather than the entire plot. Planting trenches should be 30cm (12in) wide and 30cm (12in) deep with a 15cm (6in) layer of manure or compost at the bottom. The tubers can be set directly onto the compost or manure, spaced 30cm (12in) apart. Cover the tubers and slightly mound the soil along the row. Plants grown from eyes should be planted at the same distance after the last frost on well-manured soil.

When the plants are 15-20cm (6-8in) tall, top-dress them with blood, fish and bonemeal and then earth them up by heaping the soil between the rows over the plants, leaving just a few leaves showing. Repeat this three weeks later. Potatoes need a plentiful supply of water to grow their tubers, so be sure to water regularly in dry weather. They can be harvested once they begin to flower, but only dig enough for immediate use as they will not keep well until the flowers and foliage have started to die back. Store mature potatoes in a cool, dark place in hessian or paper sacks.

Cabbage

FREEZING *does not hurt cabbages, provided you can keep them frozen; repeated thawing is what does the mischief. Therefore make a ridge 2 feet high, 6 feet wide, and as long as you need, on the north side of the building; on this lay some poles crosswise, and on the poles some narrow boards lengthwise, 2 inches apart. Take up your cabbages in a dry day, just before Winter, strip off some of the outside leaves, and set them, roots upward, on the boards, cover them a foot deep with straw or corn stalks, and they will keep fresh and green.*

THE GARDENER'S MANUAL

CABBAGE WAS AN ESSENTIAL winter vegetable for the Shakers as it kept so well throughout the winter. They grew cabbages for seed as well as for eating. *The Gardener's Manual* lists Early York, Early Sugar Loaf, Large Drumhead, Green Savoy and Red Dutch.

Because of limited space, I chose not to grow any brassicas in my Shaker garden during the first year, but the directions on growing cabbages are full of good advice, although I would add that the soil should be limed and dressed with fish, blood and bone before planting. Where cabbage root fly is a problem, cover the newly transplanted cabbages with horticultural fleece until they are well-established and growing strongly.

right **Cabbage**
The dense varieties of winter cabbages can be stored for some time if they are packed in straw and kept in a cool, vermin-free place. Alternatively they can be hung by the roots from rafters in an airy shed.

GROWING CABBAGES

For an early crop, a quantity may be sown in the hot-bed on the 10th of April, and transplanted the 10th of May, which will be the proper time for sowing the general crop. Sow in small beds, each kind by itself; sow early and late at the same time, thereby to ensure a constant succession of heads; the early furnishing a supply for Fall use, and the late holding out even till the ensuing Spring. As soon as fairly up, thin to 4 inches distance, each way; let them stand here till they have 6 leaves, then transplant. The early kinds, being small, will do at 2 feet apart each way, the late large kinds should have 3 ½ or 4 feet. Digging or ploughing between them occasionally will be highly beneficial.

THE GARDENER'S MANUAL *(1882)*

Onions, Shallots & Garlic (ONIONS):SOW

EARLY in drills, 16 inches apart and half an inch deep. Thin to 4 or 6 inches. The onions will be ripe in September.

When the tops are sufficiently dry, pull the onions, and let them lie a few days in the sun to dry; then gather them

up and house them.

THE GARDENER'S MANUAL

above

Onions

One of the best ways to store onions is to hang them in a bunch formed by twisting the un-trimmed leaves of each onion around a loop of coarse string or twine.

opposite

Onions

However you store onions, it is essential that they are fully dry or they will rot.

ONIONS

The Shakers grew large areas of onions, both for their own use and to be grown on for seed. Onion seed raised by the Enfield Shaker community was by far their most important crop and the New Lebanon gardeners make frequent references to the growing of onions in their journals. *The Gardener's Manual* lists three varieties: White Portugal, Yellow Dutch and Large Red. The Shakers boiled and baked onions and they were a common ingredient in many of their recipes.

The Shakers grew all their onions from seed, but today many gardeners prefer to grow them from sets, which can be easier and more reliable, especially in heavy soils and are also less likely to be infested by onion fly. I chose sets for my Shaker garden because I was only growing a small quantity, and I wanted to be sure that I had a full row free of any gaps.

Before planting seedlings or sets in the spring, dig in plenty of compost or well-rotted manure and top-dress with lime unless the soil is alkaline. Rake smooth and using a line as a guide, plant the sets at 10cm (4in) intervals with the tip of the bulb just below ground level. Do not push the sets into the ground or they will push themselves out by their roots as they start to grow. (Trim off old foliage at the tips to prevent birds pulling up the sets). Follow the Shaker advice on harvesting onions, making sure that they are fully ripened before bringing them indoors.

SHALLOTS

A milder, smaller version of the onion, the shallot is grown from sets and is ready earlier in the year than onions. Prepare the soil in the same way as for onions and plant the shallots in double rows with 7.5cm (3in) between the bulbs. Harvest in summer, lifting the bulbs and leaving them to dry in the same way as onions.

GARLIC

Garlic is not a vegetable that was grown by the Shakers, but it is such an essential ingredient in modern cookery that it cannot be omitted. Garlic is grown from individual cloves separated from the bulb and planted pointed end up, 2.5cm (1in) deep and 15cm (6in) apart. Prepare the soil as you would for onions and plant the cloves in late autumn or late winter. Dig the bulbs in summer and dry them in the sun before storing.

Tomatoes

This is a very healthy vegetable, and a great favourite when we become accustomed to it, though generally not very palatable at first. They should be sown in the hot-bed in April, and when the ground becomes warm, and the danger from frost is over, they may be transplanted out, 4 or 5 feet distant each way. The fruit will ripen better if the vines are supported by a trellis, or something similar, to elevate them from the ground a little.

THE GARDENER'S MANUAL

In today's world where the tomato is ubiquitous, it is extraordinary to read of the Shakers accustoming themselves to the flavour of what they clearly considered to be an exotic fruit. At the beginning of the 19th century in America, the tomato was grown as an ornamental plant and it was generally believed that the fruit were poisonous, so the Shakers were clearly pioneers when it came to tomato eating. *The Gardener's Manual* lists a variety called Large Red and instructs its readers on how to grow tomatoes and gives recipes to help them use them.

RECIPE

TOMATO CATCHUP, OR CATSUP

Collect the fruit when fully ripe, before any frost appear, squeeze or bruise them well, and boil them slowly for half an hour, then strain them through a cloth, and put in salt, pepper and spices to suit the taste. Then boil again and take off the sum that rises, so as to leave the liquor in its pure state. Keep it boiling slowly until about one half of the juice is diminished, then let it cool and put it into clear glass bottles, corked tight and kept in a cool place for use. After standing awhile, should any sediment appear in the bottles, the liquor should be poured off into other bottles and corked again tight.

THE GARDENER'S MANUAL

right

Tomatoes

Although the flavour of bought tomatoes has improved enormously, they will never compare with the flavour of a freshly picked tomato still warm from the sun. I grew three varieties in the Shaker garden – cherry tomatoes, plum tomatoes and 'beefsteak' tomatoes. A pleasing glut meant that there were plenty left over for preserving.

far right

Tomato preserve

Surplus tomatoes from the Shaker garden were preserved semi-dried in oil, bottled or as a purée.

RECIPE

PICKLED TOMATOES

Select small sized fruit, let them

lie three days in a salt pickle, drain them well, and to

half a peck of tomatoes, add half a pound of best flour of

mustard, one ounce black pepper, one half pound white

mustard seed, a small quantity of horse-radish, one

ounce of cloves, and half a dozen white onions, sliced.

No scalding is necessary – merely fill up the

jars with cold wine vinegar.

THE GARDENER'S MANUAL

Tomatoes were one of the main crops in my Shaker garden – no bought tomato can ever rival the flavor of one freshly picked from the vine. I like to grow two or three different types of outdoor tomato: cherry tomatoes for salads, and for treats as I work in the garden; plum tomatoes for making into sauces, for bottling and for semi-drying; and one of the 'beefsteak' varieties for slicing and stuffing. Next season I will grow one of the orange varieties – blindfold tests have proved that they have the fullest flavor, although the red fruit will always be chosen in preference when we can see a selection of tomatoes.

opposite

Freshly picked vine tomatoes

Don't be tempted to spoil the enjoyment of the ambrosial flavour of freshly-picked tomatoes by relegating them to the fridge – once cooled the flavour is less apparent. Good cooks will confirm that tomatoes are best kept in an open bowl at room temperature, and as the supermarkets have discovered, it helps to keep them on the vine.

Because the Shaker garden is far too popular with the slugs, I grew upright rather than bush varieties as it was easier to protect the fruit from their predations. *Tagetes* 'Harlequin' were planted between the tomatoes to encourage hoverflies and discourage aphids.

Sow outdoor tomato seed under glass in mid-spring, spacing the seeds 2.5cm (1in) apart. Prick out into 9cm (3in) pots when they have two proper leaves. Keep the plants growing strongly in good light until they are ready to be hardened off in a cold frame. Young tomato plants should be dark green, short and stocky. If they are pale green and gangly, this is a sign that they are short of food and that they should be potted on into larger pots and then given regular liquid feeds. After the last frost they can be planted out into a sunny position into moisture-retaining soil that has been enriched with compost or well-rotted manure at 60cm (2ft) spacing.

Each plant will need a sturdy stake that has been hammered firmly into position before the tomatoes are planted. A mature tomato plant covered with fruit is very heavy and will need more robust support than an ordinary garden cane. As the tomato plants grow they should be tied securely to the stake every 15cm (6in). Once four trusses of fruit have set, pinch out the growing tips and regularly remove the side shoots. Liquid feed fortnightly with seaweed or a similar organic fertiliser (see page 65 for instructions on making your own liquid feed).

(see page 65 for instructions on making your own liquid feed)

RECIPE

TOMATO & BASIL PURÉE

If you are fortunate enough to have a glut of tomatoes you could make this puree, which is excellent for sauces, soups, stews and pasta.

Ingredients

120ml (4fl oz) virgin olive oil

4 medium sized onions, finely chopped

10 large garlic cloves, chopped

6 large carrots, peeled and sliced

1 head of celery, chopped

2.25k (5lbs) very ripe tomatoes, skinned and chopped

4 large handfuls basil

half bottle of red wine

pepper and salt

5 tbsp brown sugar

2 tbsp wine vinegar

Method

Heat the oil in a large pan and gently fry the onions over a low heat until soft and golden. Add garlic, stir for 1 minute then add carrots and celery and cook till softened. Add tomatoes, basil, wine, pepper and salt and bring to the boil, then simmer uncovered for 2 hours. Blend the sauce in a food processor and then return it to the pan. Add sugar and vinegar and simmer until it has reduced by half. Cool, then freeze or bottle the sauce.

Sweetcorn

THE EARLY CANADA *is the earliest kind of corn we raise, and is preferred only for being several weeks earlier than the common field corn. The Sweet, or Sugar Corn is best for cooking in its green state, as it remains much longer in the milk, and is richer and sweeter than any other kind. It is rather later than the common field corn, and is therefore fit for the table when the field corn has become too hard. This corn may be preserved for winter use, by parboiling it when green, and cutting it from the cob and drying it in the sun. It then affords a wholesome and agreeable dish when cooked like bean porridge or what is called succotash.*

Plant on the 20th of May, in hills 4 feet distant each way. Cultivate the same as other corn, by ploughing, hilling & c.

THE GARDENER'S MANUAL

left

Corn cob

Ideally corn should be eaten within twenty minutes of being picked – after that it will never be as sweet and tender.

right

Translucent leaves

The delicate outline of a young corn plant as the morning light shines through it is evidence of how a productive garden can also be a place of beauty.

far right

Corn silk

Pick sweetcorn when the cob is plump and the silk has emerged at the point when the tips of the silk have just started to turn brown.

THE SHAKERS GREW two types of corn: common field corn for drying and grinding into maize flour and for use as a cattle feed, and sweet or sugar corn, which was eaten as a fresh vegetable, used for succotash or preserved for winter eating. Although it is described as best for cooking in its 'green' state, this does not mean that it was eaten before it was ripe, rather it was a comparison with the deeper colouring of the common field corn, the kernels of which were not as palatable due their much higher starch content and the lower level of moisture they contained.

Like potatoes, corn was grown on a field scale as it formed part of the Shakers' staple diet. It was an easier, more reliable and more productive crop than wheat. Sweetcorn was picked early. Field corn cobs were left to ripen on the plant, then harvested and the dry kernels were ground into cornmeal, which was also known as Indian meal and used to make breads and puddings, as well as animal feed.

RECIPE

MARY

WHITCHER'S

BOILED

INDIAN

PUDDING

A cupful of molasses,

one of beef suet,

chopped fine; four of

Indian meal, a little

salt, and enough

boiling water to make a

thick batter.

Tie loosely in a cloth,

and boil for two hours

or more. Serve with

butter and syrup.

The 12 sweetcorn plants in my Shaker garden were very much a token gesture – there was no room for a proper crop, but nonetheless we enjoyed a few meals of fresh corn. The corn was planted in three short rows alongside the potatoes in one of the raised beds, and though modest in number, the plants grew well and cropped prolifically.

Corn can be sown under glass or outdoors in mid-spring. Sow only one variety of corn in your garden, as growing more than one variety results in cross pollination, which reduces the sugar content. Grow corn in full sun in fertile soil. When sown under glass, corn seeds should be sown in pairs in 9cm (3in) pots and thinned to the strongest seedling. They should then be hardened off in a cold frame in late-spring before planting out in blocks rather than rows, with plants 60cm (2ft) apart after the last frost. Outdoors, dib holes 2.5cm (1in) deep and 60cm (2ft) apart in well-prepared ground in late spring and drop three seeds in each hole. Thin to one seedling at each position. Protect young plants from frost with cloches or horticultural fleece.

RECIPE

SWEETCORN   RELISH

Ingredients

8 ears of corn

1 large onion, finely chopped

1 seeded and diced red pepper

1 seeded and diced green pepper

3 diced celery stalks

225g (8oz) finely chopped green cabbage

200g (7oz) sugar

300ml (8fl oz) cider vinegar

125ml (4fl oz) water

2 teaspoons freshly ground mustard seeds

$^1/_2$ teaspoon turmeric

1 teaspoon salt

Method

Using a sharp knife cut the kernels from the cobs and scrape the milky liquid from the cobs onto the kernels. Place all the ingredients in a large non-reactive pan and bring to the boil, stirring until the sugar is dissolved. Simmer for 30 minutes, stirring occasionally. Pour into hot, sterilised jars and seal. Store in cool, dry conditions.

opposite

Corn relish

The Shakers used relishes to enliven winter meals and corn relish was one of their favourites.

Corn is sown in blocks rather than rows because it is wind pollinated and this gives the plants the best chance of good pollination. An absence of kernels on the cob is an indicator of poor fertilisation. Corn is ready for eating when the silk begins to turn brown. As soon as sweetcorn is picked, the sugar in the kernels begins to turn into starch, so to enjoy it at its best it should be cooked immediately. If you are in the happy position of having a glut of corn you can make a traditional corn relish. The Shakers used relishes and pickles to add interest to their winter diet.

above

Corn field

Corn should always be planted in blocks of plants rather than rows or it will suffer from poor pollination and this will cause gaps in the cobs.

Beans & Peas

THE RUNNING OR POLE BEANS should be planted in hills, 3½ feet distant each way. We prefer setting the poles before planting. For this purpose we stretch a line, and set the poles by it; then dig and loosen the earth, and drop five or six beans in a circle around the pole, about 3 inches from it, and cover with mellow dirt 1 inch or 1½ in depth. When the plants are well up, stir the earth around them, and pull out the weakest plants, leaving three to each hill. This should be done when they are perfectly dry; for beans never should be hoed when wet, nor when any dew is on them.

THE GARDENER'S MANUAL

above

Beans

Runner beans are at their most tender when picked young.

opposite left

Peas

Mange tout are ready to eat when the pods have reached full size, but the peas inside remain small.

opposite right

Beanpoles

A strong, tall framework of beanpoles is essential for runner beans.

opposite below

Runner beans

Stringless varieties of runner beans are more palatable and easier to prepare for cooking.

THE SHAKERS CULTIVATED both pole and bush beans. Some varieties were eaten fresh, others were preserved or dried for winter use. *The Gardener's Manual* offers two pole beans, Clapboard and Cranberry, and three bush beans, Early China, Early Purple and Early White. When eaten fresh they were generally boiled and served with butter, although *The Gardener's Manual* also recommends that after boiling young and tender beans, 'they may be made very palatable by soaking them in vinegar for a few hours.'

They also recommended that 'The green pods of beans may be kept and preserved fresh by laying them down in a jar or tub, with a layer of salt between each layer of beans.' Beans that were to be dried for winter were left to mature on the plant; once the foliage had died back the vine was uprooted and brought indoors to dry fully, after which the vines were flailed to remove the beans from the pods. *The Gardener's Manual* recommends that dried beans be soaked for 12 hours after which they should be par-boiled and then baked or stewed for 4 hours.

In my Shaker garden, having first prepared the soil by digging a trench to a spade's depth and half-filling it with well-rotted manure, I followed the example of the Shakers and put the bean poles in place before planting. This is much easier than trying to position them around the young plants, when there is a risk of damaging them. Depending on how many beans you wish to grow you can arrange the poles in a circle or in parallel lines. A circle of eight poles lashed together at the top will provide support for sufficient beans for a family of four, while parallel lines of poles can be extended indefinitely. Beans can be sown direct into the ground as directed by the Shakers, but I sowed mine indoors to avoid slug damage when the seedlings were at their most vulnerable.

KIDNEY BEANS

These are delicate plants and should not be hurried into the ground till it is well dried and warmed by the sun. The first of May is soon enough in this latitude (Albany). The dwarf or bush beans may be sown in drills, 20 inches apart, 2 inches deep, and 6 inches apart in the row.

THE GARDENER'S MANUAL

The Shakers recognised that bush beans are more delicate than pole beans and their advice to hold back planting them until the soil has warmed sufficiently is certainly worth emulating. Planted too early the seeds will rot in the soil and any that germinate will be vulnerable to cold, wet weather. This is a crop that can benefit from the use of protective cloches or horticultural fleece.

PEAS

The late and tall kinds should be sown in double drills 4 or 5 feet apart, and supported with brush. The early kinds may be sown on ridges at 3 feet distance and a foot high. This will form trenches that will carry off the water and should be kept open at the lower end. When the peas are off, every alternate trench may be prepared for celery.

THE GARDENER'S MANUAL

The Shakers had to contend with a number of difficulties with their soil. Poor drainage was a major problem in some of the communities, hence the emphasis on ridges, hills and trenches in many

above
Roots
Young plants should have a well-developed root system before they are transplanted, but should not be pot-bound.

top left
Kidney beans
Allow a few pods to ripen to provide seed for next year.

bottom left
Peas & beans
Seeds can be saved from peas and beans – allow them to dry before storing them somewhere safe from mice and insects.

of their cultivation notes. Such preparations are not needed where soil is free-draining, but in heavier soils they will produce a better crop. In summer early peas were podded and eaten fresh, sugar peas were eaten whole and main crop varieties were dried for winter use. *The Gardener's Manual* lists four types of pea: Early Washington; Early Frame; Large Marrowfat; and Tall Sugar.

Unless you have an alkaline soil, peas will benefit from a dressing of lime on the soil before planting. Stretch a line to mark the row and then use a hoe to form a trench 5cm (2in) deep. Sow the peas in staggered rows with the peas 2.5cm (1in) apart. Cover the peas with soil and press down firmly with the back of a rake. To protect them from marauding mice, cover the rows with fine gauge wire mesh until the plants emerge. Push pea brush in place along the rows to give support to the growing plants. If bird damage is likely to be a problem, wind fine black cotton among the brush to discourage them. Nowadays peas are generally eaten fresh, and to taste their best they should be picked before they are fully mature when they become less sweet.

After peas and beans have finished cropping cut the plants back to ground level, but leave the roots in place as they are rich in nitrogen that they will slowly release into the soil.

Salads

VARIOUS SALADS *are mentioned in* The Gardener's Manual *but there is little reference to how they ate them. Six varieties of lettuce are listed: Early Imperial, Early Curled, Early Dutch, Ice Coss, Cabbage-head and Frankfort, and it describes peppergrass (curled cress) as making 'an agreeable salad'. The Shakers believed that 'crisp' celery was good for the nerves and* The Gardener's Manual *gives long and detailed instructions on how to grow this very demanding crop, involving hot beds, trenches, earthing up and much else. It is not an easy crop to grow successfully, especially among other crops, so I did not grow it in the Shaker garden, choosing instead to include less labour intensive salads such as rocket and spinach.*

CUCUMBER

The 20th of May is soon enough to plant cucumbers here. Hills to be 4 feet distant each way. One plant is enough for a hill, ultimately; but to make provision for insects, plenty of seed should be put in, and the plants afterwards thinned out.

THE GARDENER'S MANUAL

The Shakers grew cucumbers in hot beds and frames and hardier varieties outdoors on hills. These days there are plenty of varieties that are suitable for outdoor cultivation. Start young plants under glass or sow seeds in pairs in rich deeply-cultivated soil. Train the cucumber plants up poles, tying them in place frequently and pinching out side-shoots to two leaves to keep the plants compact. Pinch out the growing tips when the plants reach the top of the poles. Water frequently and liquid feed weekly. Cucumbers, with their very high water content, will taste bitter if deprived of water. To enjoy them at their best, pick the cucumbers while there is still a bloom on the skin. In parts of America the cucumber beetle can be a problem – late sowing avoids the worst damage. Wood ash around the base of the plant is a deterrent as is interplanting with tagetes.

below
Young lettuce

Young lettuce ready for transplanting into the garden – any thinnings can be enjoyed as an early salad.

opposite
Lettuce

Packets of mixed lettuce seed are available that allow the gardener to enjoy a variety of lettuce.

below right
Cos lettuce

The small varieties of cos lettuce such as 'Little Gem' are ideal where space is limited.

LETTUCE

Sow as early as possible in the Spring, and at intervals through the season, in drills 1 foot apart and $^1/_2$ an inch deep. The early kinds need but little thinning; but head Lettuce should stand 8 or 10 inches apart, or they will have but inferior heads, and if very thick, none at all.

THE GARDENER'S MANUAL

Like radishes, lettuces should be sown little and often to ensure a regular supply, or if your requirements are small you can grow one of the cut-and-come-again varieties. In my Shaker garden where space was very limited, I sowed lettuces in boxes and later transplanted them wherever space was available among the other crops.

PEPPERS

'These should be sown in the hot bed in April, and transplanted out the 1st of June, 2 feet distant each way.' *The Gardener's Manual* lists three varieties of pepper: Squash, Sweet Bell and Large Bell. The Sweet Bell was 'commonly used, when fully ripe, as a salad; or the core may be extracted and the cavity filled with mince meat, which, on being thus baked, receives a very agreeable relish.'

In the absence of a hot bed, I started my peppers under glass and planted them out after the last frost, on ground that had been further warmed by cloches. The soil was well manured and I planted them in full sunshine in a sheltered corner. Peppers need plenty of water and a weekly feed with liquid fertiliser. Pinch out the growing tip of the plants when they reach 20cm (8in) to encourage productive side shoots.

RADISHES

'Sow and cultivate the same as onions. As they soon become too old for the table, they should be sown once a fortnight, in order to have a supply through the season.' *The Gardener's Manual* lists a number of radishes, both salad varieties, including Short Top Scarlet and larger winter radishes including a variety called Black Winter. Radishes are among the easiest of all salad vegetables to grow, but the Shakers are quite right in recommending regular sowings: 'a freshly picked young radish is a delight – an old one has little to recommend it.' In my Shaker Garden I sowed 60cm (2ft) rows at regular intervals wherever space permitted. This gave a moderate supply of radishes without necessitating eating them every day!

SPINACH

Although listed in *The Gardener's Manual* as 'Spinage, Roundleaf' there are no instructions on how to grow it or how to cook it. It is an easy and quick-growing vegetable that does best in rich soil and partial shade – full sun will make it run to seed prematurely. Sow monthly through the growing season in shallow drills 30cm (12in) apart. Thin the plants to intervals of 15cm (6in).

ROCKET

Although rocket was not a Shaker salad, I included it in my garden because it is so delicious, so easy to grow and no modern vegetable garden should be without it. Where space is very limited it can be even grown in seed trays or boxes. It is not fussy about soil conditions, can be sown from mid-spring onwards (earlier under cloches) and once it has germinated it will grow happily with no further attention. Cut it when it is 15cm (6in) high, and re-sow at regular intervals for a continuous supply.

above
Rocket
Rocket by name, rocket by nature – this is a salad which grows very, very fast. Pick it young.

opposite
Radish
Sow radishes regularly throughout the summer and eat them often.

Esteemed vegetables

AFTER THE INITIAL *hungry years, the Shakers gained a reputation for the quality of their food, which was frequently praised by observers from 'the World'. Like other Americans of the period – and ever since – they were given to experimenting with popular dietary trends including vegetarianism, which was adopted to a greater or lesser extent by the Shaker communities. Among the more everyday vegetables, the Shakers looked forward to, and greatly enjoyed, some of the less commonplace treats that seasonally graced their tables.* The Gardener's Manual *lists asparagus, egg plant (aubergine) and sea kale among the vegetable seed they offered for sale.*

ARTICHOKE

The artichoke is not referred to by the Shakers, but it would certainly have ranked as a special treat had they grown it in their vegetable gardens. In milder regions it can be grown as a perennial, but the most productive way to grow it is from side shoots newly planted each year in mid spring. Artichokes need deeply-cultivated, rich, moisture-retaining soil in a sunny, sheltered part of the garden where the shoots should be planted with 1m (3ft) between plants. Pick the artichokes while still quite tightly closed. Cut the plants back to 30cm (12in) after fruiting and mulch with manure if they are to be overwintered.

ASPARAGUS

This is a very delicious esculent vegetable, and easily cultivated, after the first operation of preparing the ground. Prepare your bed by working a plentiful supply of strong manure into the ground, to the depth of 18 inches. Level the top of the bed, stretch your line, and with a hoe, shovel, or plough, mark out drills 6 inches deep, and 2 feet apart. In these drills, or rather furrows, set the asparagus roots 20 inches asunder; these roots will spread, and in a few years, asparagus will shoot up in every part of

above

Asparagus

The Shakers were very partial to asparagus which they described as an 'esculent vegetable' – in other words they found it delicious.

opposite

Baby artichoke

The globe artichoke is not difficult to grow and should be included in every garden, space permitting.

the bed. When the setting out is completed, level the top of the bed and let it grow up. Every succeeding Spring the stalks should be cut up, and hauled off or burned on the ground. The buds or young shoots, which is the part used, will be fit for cutting the third year; they should be cut sparingly the first year, but thereafter, the cutting may be continued until the first of July, when a coat of dung should be spread on and turned under, and the asparagus suffered to run up to seed.

THE GARDENER'S MANUAL

Asparagus plants are bought as 'crowns' (roots), which should be soaked overnight, then planted in trenches with a raised mound along the middle so that the growing tip is raised above the roots. The soil should be well-manured and dressed with lime and fish, blood and bone. Remove the yellowing foliage in autumn to discourage pests and diseases, and add a protective mulch of well-rotted manure or compost.

EGG PLANT (AUBERGINE)

Plant them out towards the latter part of May, in a rich, warm piece of ground, in rows 3 feet apart, and at the distance of 2 feet in the rows. They bear fruit when about 1 foot high, which if rightly prepared, is by many esteemed to be equal to eggs. Some are very fond of them when sliced and fried with ham.

THE GARDENER'S MANUAL

The Shakers sowed their egg plants in hot beds in the middle of March, and avoided planting them out until the soil was thoroughly warmed. Egg plants need a sunny sheltered location and well-manured soil, top-dressed with lime if it is acid. Stake the plants and tie in place. Allow five fruits to set on each plant and remove any other flowers once the fruit have set. Feed weekly with a liquid fertiliser. Pick the fruit when they are rigid and shiny, left on the plant they will develop a bitter taste.

RECIPE

FRIED EGG

PLANT

Cut into slices about a quarter of an inch thick, put them into a dish, and pour on boiling water, let them remain a minute or two; drain off the water, and season with pepper and salt, or with thyme, marjoram, or summer savory, according to the palate to be suited; dust them with flour and put them into a frying pan, which should be ready with hot beef drippings, or lard. When browned on one side, turn them and brown the other.

THE GARDENER'S MANUAL

opposite

Egg plant (aubergine)

The Egg Plant or Aubergine was one of the more exotic crops cultivated by the Shakers. They carefully nurtured them in hot beds until it was warm enough to plant them outdoors.

left

Ruby Chard

Ruby Chard is both decorative and delicious. It also lasts well into the winter and in milder areas will continue growing until spring.

RUBY CHARD

This vegetable is in my Shaker garden in the spirit of Shaker innovation. Although there is no reference to it in *The Gardener's Manual* I believe that this vegetable embodies 'useful beauty' with its stunning leaf and stem colouring and its tasty leaves, which can be included uncooked in salads when young and cooked like spinach when mature. It is also one of the longest lasting vegetables in the garden producing leaves from early summer through to winter. Grow ruby chard in rich, moisture retentive, alkaline soil (top-dress with lime if necessary). Sow seeds in mid-spring in rows 35cm (15in) apart. Thin seedlings to 30cm (12in). Harvest ruby chard by pulling the outer leaves from the plant – do not cut them as this will cause the plant to bleed.

SEA KALE

This is a capital article; the cultivation and use are the same as those of Asparagus. Break the shells before sowing.

THE GARDENER'S MANUAL

This is a vegetable that is seldom grown these days, and although pleasant enough to eat when blanched, the effort and space required to cultivate it were beyond the scope of myself and my modest Shaker garden. Root crowns are sometimes available from specialist growers.

Companion Planting

We tested the plan of strewing tomato vines under plum trees, as a preventative of the curculio; and on a tree that we have invariably lost all, or nearly every plum, we had a nice quantity of the most beautiful fruit. We shall practise this simple provision.

The Shaker Manifesto *(1878)*

There is a long tradition of companion planting that has been passed on through generations of gardeners and the Shakers certainly practised some aspects of it in their gardens. With their scrupulous record-keeping they would have been in a good position to comment on which associations were effective and which were simply folklore, but unfortunately I could find only the above observation on this subject.

Companion planting is carried out for three reasons. Firstly, it has been found that certain plants have insect-repelling properties and can usefully be used to protect crops from attack. Secondly, the inclusion of plants that attract beneficial predator insects can control damage, and thirdly, it is believed that some plant combinations have a symbiotic effect on the growth of the plants concerned, i.e. they appear to grow better and healthier than when grown separately.

Of all companion plants, the French marigold *tagetes* is the most effective insect repellent. In my Shaker garden I grew an old-fashioned variety called 'Harlequin'. This plant dates back to the 1870's and is a tall-growing variety with stunning flowers striped alternately red and yellow. Planted in among the tomatoes its strong scent acts as a deterrent to aphids. If planted among cabbages it will deter cabbage white butterflies and the secretions from its roots effectively control eelworm damage to potatoes. Carrots are traditionally grown alongside onions to deter both carrot root fly and onion fly. There is little evidence that this is effective against carrot fly as carrots need a physical barrier to keep root fly at bay – a screen or a covering of horticultural fleece has been shown to be more effective.

Planting to attract beneficial insects is good common sense. Aromatic herbs will lure bees into the garden and both types of marigold – *tagetes* and *calendula* – are attractive to hoverflies, as are poppies and nasturtiums. When it comes to symbiotic planting, borage is believed to benefit strawberries. Growing sweetcorn and potatoes together is supposed to improve both crops, while chervil planted alongside radishes is reputed to make the radishes taste hotter. This aspect of companion planting is the most questionable as there are so many variable factors such as climate, position and soil condition that also influence how a plant grows.

top right
Onion & carrot
Planting carrots and onions next to one another is meant to deter carrot fly. In my experience a physical barrier is the only real deterrent.

bottom right
Tomato & tagetes
The tagetes daisy is an effective deterrent to aphids, while its bright colours attract welcome beneficial insects.

far right
Potato & corn
When potatoes and sweetcorn grow alongside one another both crops are said to grow better.

"They *consume* much fruit,

eating it at every meal.**"**

Charles Nordhoff, *Communistic Societies of the United States 1875*

fruit

Fragaria x

Melons, and other choice *or uncommon fruits, should be equally divided to the family, as far as consistent; and no member should raise or gather them – to give to particular individuals to court favor or affection.*

THE MILLENNIAL LAWS *(1845)*

IT IS A MEASURE of how rare a treat they must have been if melons were seen as a potentially corrupting influence by the Shakers. It would have taken all the skill of the New England Shaker gardeners to rear melons in hot beds, and once planted out, poor weather could easily have ruined the crop. In the days before fruit was regularly shipped from warmer climates, northern communities would have had little other opportunity to taste this fruit, although watermelon was much eaten at South Union, Kentucky. Perhaps because of this, another Millennial Law states that 'Believers may not spend their time cultivating fruits and plants, not adapted to the climate in which they live.'

opposite
A wealth of produce

Shaker gardens were unsurpassed at one time, fruit and vegetables were grown in prodigious quantities to feed the Shakers and to be sold.

Bearing in mind the extra time and effort required to successfully grow crops outside their natural climate, this is sound advice for all but the most dedicated and enthusiastic gardener. Nevertheless, the Shaker gardeners were great experimenters, continually grafting and testing new varieties to ascertain what did and did not grow successfully in their particular conditions, and there were plenty of fruits that they ate in abundance.

Apples, pears, quinces, peaches, cherries and berries, depending on the climate of a community, were a regular part of their diet, either eaten fresh, or stored, preserved, or dried for eating out of season. Soft fruit was also made into ice cream – at North Union the Shakers built an icehouse in 1874 to store the ice that they cut from their lakes during the winter, and a motorised ice-cream maker was one of the many Shaker inventions for the kitchen.

The mechanical apple peeler was another, which must have been very welcome in the Shaker kitchens where a glut of apples was an annual event that required the entire community to lend a hand in harvesting, preparing and drying much of the crop and making applesauce, which was eaten daily at one meal or another. The fruit cheeses, jellies, pies and preserves made in the community kitchens also found a ready market with visitors from 'the World' who came to visit the Shaker villages, drawn by the superior quality of the goods and produce available.

Soft Fruit

FRAGRANT PUFFS *of boiling fruit and spices emanated from the basement kitchen and filled the halls.*

VISITOR TO SABBATHDAY LAKE, 1910 – THE FOUR SEASONS OF SHAKER LIFE

STRAWBERRIES

The immodestly named 'Great Austin Shaker Seedling Strawberry, the Largest Strawberry in the World' described as 'remarkable for flavour as for size and thrift' with berries that were claimed to measure 5 inches, was one of the varieties bred by the Shakers and offered for sale in their seed catalogues. Strawberries were a favourite summer fruit for the Shakers, and were often mentioned in daily journals when served. They undoubtedly tested this and many other varieties for the community gardeners. These days we are suspicious of overlarge fruit and vegetables, fearing that flavour has been sacrificed for size. A well-flavoured 5 inch strawberry sounds too good to be true – and it has to be said that some Shaker advertising made claims that would not be countenanced today.

I planted a row of strawberries in one of the raised beds in my Shaker garden, selecting a variety that bears more moderate sized berries of good flavour. Strawberries do best in well-drained fertile soil, enriched with compost or manure, in a sunny spot with good air circulation to cut down on mildew problems. They were traditionally planted in late summer to crop the following year, but cold-stored plants are now available, which can be planted out between May and July to crop the same year. Plant strawberries firmly into soil worked down to a fine tilth, ensuring that the roots go straight down into the hole, and that the final

top left

Strawberries

A straw mulch prevents the berries being splashed with soil and also helps to keep the fruit dry.

centre

Strawberry in flower

Water flowering strawberry plants well to ensure a good set of fruit.

right

Soft fruit preserve

Home-made jams are the perfect solution when dealing with a glut of soft fruit.

planting depth has the roots fully covered and the crown above soil level.

Once planted, if any of the plants fail to thrive, remove the first flowers to encourage better root and leaf development. As the fruit sets it needs to be lifted above the ground. Straw is the traditional way to do this, and looks more attractive than plastic. I protected the ripening fruit from marauding birds with individual bamboo cloches, which looked just right in the Shaker garden, but netting can also be used. After harvesting the fruit, cut back the foliage within 2.5cm (1in) of the crown and compost it along with the straw mulch. Apply a dressing of rock potash. As new foliage develops, runners will be sent out from the plant. Choose the best and root into pots of compost whilst they are still attached to the mother plant. The strawberry bed should be replanted after two years of cropping for maximum productivity. If you have access to pine needles strawberries love them as a mulch.

RECIPE

SOFT FRUIT JAM

Jam sugar with added pectin dramatically cuts down on the time it takes to make jams.

Ingredients

1kg (2¼lb) soft fruit

600ml (1 pint) cloudy apple juice

1kg (2¼lb) sugar with pectin

Method

Place the fruit and the apple juice in a heavy pan and bring to the boil. Simmer for 5 mintutes, stirring gently,. Add the sugar, stir until dissolved. Boil briskly for 4 minutes, leave to stand for 15 minutes and then pour into warm, dry jars.

CURRANTS & GOOSEBERRIES

The reference to rhubarb being ready earlier than currants and goose berries indicates that these berries were also grown by the Shakers. As each bush needs an area 1.5m (5ft) square, they are only suitable for larger gardens and although both currants and gooseberries are delicious, they are susceptible to a variety of pests and diseases so I have not included them in my Shaker garden.

below

Gooseberries

The gooseberry is an often under-rated soft fruit. The dessert varieties which ripen to a rich golden-yellow or dark red are delicious eaten raw. Cooked gooseberries develop a muscat flavour if elderflowers are added.

right

Blackcurrants

Blackcurrants are not an ideal crop for growing in a small garden as they develop into fairly large bushes, but space permitting, it is well worth growing this delicious fruit, which is also rich in vitamin C .

left

Blackberry flowers

Wild blackberry plants are so thorny that it can be difficult to get close enough to admire the delicate beauty of the flowers.

right

Blackberries

Ripe blackberries in the Shaker garden. The thornless varieties are much easier to train and control – and the fruit is just as delicious.

BLACKBERRIES

The blackberry is a favourite autumn fruit of cool regions, which would have been gathered wild and eaten fresh or made into pies or jelly by the Shakers. These days the thornless varieties make it a suitable plant for cultivation and I planted two vines against the picket fence in my Shaker garden. The soil was enriched with plenty of composted manure and a sprinkling of bonemeal. Allow 3m (10ft) between plants, and cut the stems back to 15cm (6in) after planting. Vine eyes were screwed into the fence, with wires threaded through parallel to the ground at 60cm (24in), and 30cm (12in) intervals to the top of the fence. Tie the briars to the wires as they grow. After you have picked the crop, cut the harvested briars to ground level and tie in the new growths ready for next year's crop.

BLUEBERRIES

The Shakers harvested blueberries from the wild during the 19th century to use as a flavouring for medicines and for cooking. Blueberries need acid soil and are a long-term commitment, taking three to eight years to bear fruit. They are not self-fertile, so more than one variety must be planted. Plant in autumn into soil enriched with manure and bonemeal, and mulch and top-dress annually.

RASPBERRIES

Raspberry canes do best on heavy, rich soil planted in autumn into a trench on a layer of manure dressed with bonemeal. Plant canes slightly deeper than the soil mark on the stems and cut them back to 15cm (6in). Tie new growth to parallel wires attached to 1.5m (5ft) posts at either end of the trench. The canes should be 10cm (4in) apart. Cut back the growing tips 10cm (4in) above the top wire. Once the fruit has been picked, cut the old canes to ground level and select the strongest new growths and tie them in place. Net to protect ripening fruit from the birds.

RECIPE

RASPBERRY VINEGAR

To two quarts of raspberries put one pint of cider vinegar. After two or three days mash the fruit and strain through a bag. To every pint allow a pound of sugar. Boil twenty minutes and skim. Bottle when cold. Makes a pleasant drink put into water.

MARY WHITCHER'S SHAKER HOUSE-KEEPER *(1882)*

Rhubarb

SOW THE FIRST YEAR *very early in drills, 2 feet apart and 1 inch in depth. Thin to 10 inches. The second year transplant them out 4 feet distant each way. Shade them from the hot sun, both the first and second year, till they gain good roots. The seed stalks should not be suffered to grow. The stalks or stems of the leaves, cut up and prepared, are as good for pies as currants or gooseberries, and six weeks earlier. The roots are used in medicine.*

THE GARDENER'S MANUAL

RHUBARB IS A VERY PROLIFIC crop once it is fully established, and if it was being grown on a large scale by the Shakers to provide dried roots for medical purposes, this would explain why *The Gardener's Manual* went to some lengths to give suitable recipes. They must have had an awful lot of rhubarb! One or two rhubarb plants are ample for most households.

Plant crowns in late autumn, or pot-grown plants at any time of year, into enriched free-draining soil with a dressing of lime for acid soils. Allow 1m (3ft) square for each plant. Do not cut or pull any leaves the first year. Cut back remaining foliage in late autumn and top-dress with plenty of compost or well-rotted manure. In early spring, cover plants with a forcer or large pot to 'force' the new shoots, which will be pale pink, tender and delicious.

The Shaker Sisters baked a prodigious numbers of pies, and from its common name 'Pie Plant', rhubarb must have featured regularly in their repertoire. This recipe from *The Gardener's Manual* could help you with your own rhubarb glut!

RECIPE

RHUBARB PIE

Peel and wash one or two dozen sticks of Rhubarb; put them in a stew pan, with the peel of a lemon, a bit of cinnamon, two cloves, and as much moist sugar as will sweeten it; set it over a fire, and reduce it to a marmalade, pass it through a hair sieve; then add the peel of a lemon and half a nutmeg grated, a quarter of a pound of good butter, and the yolks of 4 eggs and one white, and mix well all together; line a pie dish, that will just contain it, with a good puff paste, put the mixture in, and bake it half an hour.

left
Rhubarb
Rhubarb is best picked young and most delicious when the young growth is forced by covering the crowns early in the year. Old stems are sharper in taste, coarser in texture and generally less appealing. The leaves of the rhubarb plant are poisonous and must not be eaten.

Orchard Fruit

A TREE HAS ITS WANTS *and wishes and a man*

should study it as a teacher watches a child, to see what he can do. I don't know if a tree comes to know you;

and I think it may; but I am sure it feels when you care for it and tend it, as a child does, as a woman does.

Now when we planted this orchard, we first got the very best cuttings in our reach; we then built a house for

every plant to live in, that is to say, we dug a deep hole for each; we drained it well; we laid down tiles and

rubble, and then filled in a bed of suitable manure and mould; we put the plant into its nest gently, and pressed

the earth about it; and protected the infant tree by this metal fence.

HEPWORTH DIXON – THE PEOPLE CALLED SHAKERS

RECIPE

DRIED APPLE RINGS

Thinly slice crisp apples and immerse

the slices in a mixture made up of

equal parts of lemon juice and of water.

Thread onto skewers and leave to

dry in a warm airy space

THIS BEAUTIFUL DESCRIPTION of planting an orchard has me longing to rush out and plant an orchard of my own – not with semi-mature trees as is the general habit of today, but with young saplings that I can nurture to full and productive growth. It is clear that the speaker is describing how a mature orchard came into being and he speaks with real affection for the trees; his description of the preparations involved in preparing a 'nest' for each young tree should be emulated by anyone who plans to plant a tree.

An orchard is a long-term commitment, not something to be rushed at, so it is worth spending plenty of time preparing the ground and choosing varieties that are suitable for your purposes and will thrive in your local conditions. Contact a specialist grower rather than buying the young trees from your local garden centre – you will get a better choice and superior trees. Although fruit trees can be bought grown in pots, they are less expensive and will often establish better if they are bought bare-rooted from late autumn to early spring. They can be planted at any time during this period, provided the soil is not waterlogged or frozen. Holes can be dug and prepared ahead of time and covered with a waterproof cover. Before planting the young tree, knock a strong stake firmly in position and then attach the tree to it using a proper tree-tie, which can be adjusted as the tree grows. Keep the base of the trunk weed-free.

left

Pear

Like most orchard fruit, pear trees can be bought that have been trained into different shapes – standard, half standard, fan, cordon and step-over – and grown to different sizes, to suit any size of garden.

below

Cherries

One of the most delicious orchard fruits – but very vulnerable to poor weather and birds. Risky to grow, but well worth a try.

above

Apple

Choose your apple varieties carefully – after all, you will be eating them for many years to come so they had better be a variety you enjoy.

right

Quince

The quince is one of the prettiest orchard trees, producing lovely pale pink flowers followed by mellow golden fruit which have a delicious flavour when cooked.

right

**Apple orchard –
Canterbury Shaker
village**

*Before your plant an
orchard you should give
some thought to what
you will do with all the
fruit. A single apple tree
can be very prolific while
a whole orchard can
become a nightmare
unless you have animals
you can feed with the
windfalls and plenty of
time to store and
preserve the crop.*

Once the trees have been planted they will need continued care. In the early years they should be watered generously in very dry weather. It is wise to thin heavy crops on young trees to prevent the weight of the growing fruit breaking the branches. Clear grass and vegetation from around the base of the tree, as they will compete for nutrients. There should be at least 1m (3ft) diameter of bare earth. Top-dress around the tree with bonemeal in the autumn and cover the soil with a generous mulch of well-rotted manure or compost.

Few of us have space for a full-size orchard, but dwarfing root stock means that we can grow at least one of our favourite orchard fruits in most gardens. Fan-trained, cordon-trained or

step-over trees can be planted against a wall or alongside a path – useful beauty that would have the approval of the Shakers. Pruning fruit trees is not difficult, but it does depend on the type of fruit and the type of tree so it is not really possible to give generalised advice on this matter. Ask for advice or a leaflet from the grower who sold you the trees.

Try to select varieties that are specifically mentioned as being disease resistant. This is important for the organic grower who does not use the chemicals that are used on commercial orchards. I am not sure what type of caterpillars the Shakers are referring to in the extract above, nor exactly what a Pickering brush is, but it is typical of the ingenious way the Shakers worked.

Apples

ABOUT THE NICEST MORSEL *that ever tickled the palate is a boiled apple; not boiled like a potato nor steamed like a dumpling, but as follows; Place a layer of fair-skinned Baldwins, or any other nice varieties, in a stew-pan, with about a quarter of an inch of water. Throw on about half a cup of sugar to six good-sized apples, and boil until the apples are thoroughly cooked and the syrup nearly thick enough for jelly. After one trial no one would, for any consideration, have fair-skinned apples peeled. The skins contain a very large share of the jelly-making substance, and impart a flavour impossible to obtain otherwise.*

MARY WHITCHER'S SHAKER HOUSE-KEEPER *(1882)*

RECIPE

APPLE JELLY

Ingredients

Apple pulp (cooked, chopped apples)

Preserving sugar

Method

Strain the pulp overnight through a jelly bag. For every 500ml (1 pint) of liquid add 500g (1lb) of preserving sugar. Boil rapidly until setting point is reached, then pour into warmed jars and seal.

THE SHAKERS LOVED their most widely planted fruit tree, the apple. Initially many were grown for cider, but even after these were grubbed up to discourage cider-making, apples were still grown for eating fresh, drying and processing. Apple pies flavoured with rose-water were a favourite among the communities and also sold readily, as did their applesauce that was sold to 'the World' for over 50 years. The apple harvest was a time of community celebration much enjoyed by all who took part from the oldest to the youngest.

The apple was brought to America by early settlers along with other orchard fruits. Pears, plums, cherries and quinces were all grown and enjoyed by the Shakers. Of these fruit only the quince is relatively little grown today, which is a great shame as it is a decorative tree with beautiful flowers. The heavy golden fruit impart a wonderful flavour to apples when they are cooked together and a freshly picked quince has a fragrance that will scent an entire room. It can be pruned to a mop-head tree to fit into most small gardens. When other orchard fruit are readily available from the shops and there is space for only one tree, grow one that looks lovely and will present you with a crop not easily available elsewhere. Useful beauty yet again.

The gentler climate of the more southerly Shaker communities also allowed gardeners to grow less hardy fruit such as peaches and apricots, and for a brief period when there was a settlement in Florida, Shakers were even growing their own oranges.

On my year's journey, as I laid out my garden, grew my plants and wrote this book, it became clear to me that in their mission to 'create a heaven on earth' the Shaker gardeners approached each task with a love, diligence and intelligence from which the modern Shaker gardener can draw much help and inspiration. I hope I have done them justice.

opposite
Storing apples

*Choose only
unblemished apples.
Wrap each one in a nest
of paper and pack the
fruit in a single layer on
a tray or shelf. Check
from time to time and
remove any which are
deteriorating.*

left
Apple jelly

*To make apple jelly
begin by roughly
chopping apples,
including the core and
skin. Place them in a
heavy pan, just covering
them with water and
boil until they are soft.
Strain the resulting pulp
then follow the recipe on
the opposite page.*

Suppliers

ACCESSORIES

CLOCHES

Andrew Crace

Bourne Lane,

Much Hadham,

Hertfordshire

SG10 6ER

Tel: 01279 842685 fax: 01279 843646

DOLLY TUB AND TOOLS

Ann Lingard

Rope Walk Antiques

Rye

Sussex

TN31 7NA

Tel: 01797 223 486 fax: 01797 224700

HIVE STORE

Forsham Cottage Arks

Goreside Farm

Great Chart, Ashford,

Kent

TN26 1JU

Tel: 01233 820229 fax 01233 820157

PAINTS

Heritage Village Colours

U.K. Supplier

The Old Village Paint Store

Shop 3, Heart of the Country

Home Farm, Swinfen WS14 9QR

Tel: 01543 480 669

U.S. SUPPLIER

GRYPHIN CO. INC

3501 Richmond Street

Philadelphia

PA19134

Tel: (215) 426 5976

ORGANIC SEEDS

Terre de Semences

Ripple Farm

Crundale

Canterbury

Kent CT4 7EB

Tel: 01227 731815 and 0966 448379

THE SHAKER SHOP — ENGLAND

THE SHAKER SHOP

322 Kings Road

London SW3 5UH

Tel: 0171 352 3918

AND

72-73 Marylebone High Street

London W1M 3AR

Tel: 0171 935 9461 (also for mail order)

Fax: 0171 935 4157 (for mail order)

www.shaker.co.uk

right

Farm cart

A farm cart awaits the horses at a Shaker settlement.

Index

Numbers in *italic* refer to picture captions

Bibliography

THE GARDENER'S MANUAL (1843)
Facsimile edition reprinted from the library at Hancock Shaker Village, Hancock, Massachusetts 1991

THE EARTH SHALL BLOSSOM
Galen Beale & Mary Rose Boswell (The Countryman Press, Inc. Woodstock, Vermont) 1991

THE SHAKER HERB & GARDEN BOOK
Rita Buchanan (Houghton Mifflin & Company) 1996

SHAKER – THE ART OF CRAFTSMANSHIP
Timothy D Rieman (Art Services International, Alexandria, Virginia) 1995

SHAKER, LIFE, WORK, AND ART
June Sprigg and David Larkin (Cassell Publishers Ltd, London) 1988

IN A SHAKER KITCHEN
Norma MacMillan (Pavilion Books Ltd. London) 1995

SIMPLE GIFTS
June Sprigg (Vintage Books New York) 1998

Acknowledgements

SHAKER VILLAGES AND ORGANISATIONS

HANCOCK SHAKER VILLAGE

P O Box 927

Pittsfield, MA 01202

Tel:413 447 9357

www.shakerworkshops.com/hancock.htm

CANTERBURY SHAKER VILLAGE

288 Shaker Road,

Canterbury, NH 03224

Tel: (800) 982 9511

www.shakers.org/index.shtml

THE SHAKER LIBRARY

Sabbathday Lake

707 Shaker Road

New Gloucester, ME 04260

Tel: (207) 926 4597

www.shakerworkshops.com/sdl.htm

THE SHAKER MUSEUM & LIBRARY

88 Shaker Museum Road

Old Chatham, NY 12136

Tel: (518) 794 9100

www.shakerworkshops.com/sml.htm

SHAKER MUSEUM

at South Union, Kentucky

P O Box 30

South Union, KY 42283

Tel: (800) 811 8379

www.logantele.com/~shakmus/index.htm

SHAKER VILLAGE OF PLEASANT HILL

3501 Lexington Road

Harrodsburg, KY 40330

Tel: (800) 734 5611

www.shakervillageky.org/info.html

ENFIELD SHAKER MUSEUM

2 Lower Shaker Village

Enfield, NH 03748

Tel: (603) 632 4346

www.shakerworkshops.com/lsv.htm

SHAKER HERITAGE SOCIETY

1848 Shaker Meeting House

Albany Shaker Road

Albany, NY 12211

Tel: (518) 456 7890

www.shakerworkshops.com/waterv.htm

UNITED KINGDOM

THE AMERICAN MUSEUM IN BRITAIN

Claverton Manor

Bath, BA2 7BD

Tel: 01225 460503

THE AUTHOR WOULD LIKE TO THANK THE FOLLOWING PEOPLE FOR THEIR CONTRIBUTION TO THIS BOOK:

The team who ensured that producing this book was a happy experience: Anna Mumford *(commissioning editor)*, Jane Trollope *(editor)*, Michelle Garrett *(photographer)*, Debbie Mole *(designer)*, Gabrielle Izen *(illustrator)* • Martyn Saunders & Kathe Deutsch *for allowing me free reign in their garden* • Stewart Walton *for his skills in making the birdhouse* • Jack & Debbie Howell *for doing the hard landscaping for the Shaker Garden* • Sally Morse Majewski and Sharon Duane Koomler from the Hancock Shaker Village *for their help and advice* • Raymond Bradshaw, *The Old Village Paint Store for generously providing all the paint for the book* • Ann Lingard *for the loan of tools for photography* • Forsham Cottage Arks *for the loan of the beehive store*

DEDICATION:

This book is dedicated to the Shakers and especially to the Sister who *'did not want to be remembered as a chair'*.